ONE + ONE

HATS

ONE + ONE

HATS

30 PROJECTS FROM JUST TWO SKEINS

IRIS SCHREIER

LARK CRAFTS

Asheville

Editor
Beth Sweet

Art Director
Shannon Yokeley

Book Designer
Celia Naranjo

Illustrator
Orrin Lundgren

Photographer
Lynne Harty

Cover Designer
Shannon Yokeley

LARK CRAFTS

An Imprint of Sterling Publishing
387 Park Avenue South
New York, NY 10016

If you have questions or comments about
this book, please visit: larkcrafts.com

Library of Congress Cataloging-in-Publication Data

Schreier, Iris.
  One + one : hats : 30 projects from just two skeins / Iris Schreier. -- 1st ed.
    p. cm.
  Includes bibliographical references and index.
  ISBN 978-1-4547-0317-4 (alk. paper)
  1. Knitting--Patterns. 2. Hats. I. Title. II. Title: One plus one : hats.
  TT825.S3926 2012
  746.43'2--dc23

                    2011047740

10 9 8 7 6 5 4 3 2 1

First Edition

Published by Lark Crafts
An Imprint of Sterling Publishing Co., Inc.
387 Park Avenue South, New York, NY 10016

Text © 2012, Iris Schreier
Photography © 2012, Lark Crafts, an Imprint of Sterling Publishing Co., Inc.
Illustrations © 2012, Lark Crafts, an Imprint of Sterling Publishing Co., Inc.

Distributed in Canada by Sterling Publishing, c/o Canadian Manda Group,
165 Dufferin Street, Toronto, Ontario, Canada M6K 3H6

Distributed in the United Kingdom by GMC Distribution Services,
Castle Place, 166 High Street, Lewes, East Sussex, England BN7 1XU

Distributed in Australia by Capricorn Link (Australia) Pty Ltd.,
P.O. Box 704, Windsor, NSW 2756 Australia

Manufactured in China

ISBN 13: 978-1-4547-0317-4

For information about custom editions, special sales, premium and corporate purchases, please
contact Sterling Special Sales Department at 800-805-5489 or specialsales@sterlingpub.com.

For information about desk and examination copies available to college and university professors,
requests must be submitted to academic@larkbooks.com. Our complete policy can be found at
www.larkcrafts.com.

contents

CABLES AND BOBBLES

SIDE-TO-SIDE AND BIAS

DOUBLE KNIT

introduction

ONE of the hardest things for knitters is to figure out how to mix colors and yarns in their knitting. But that is sometimes what we have the most fun with, since working with different colors and textures keeps the knitting so interesting.

One + One Hats is the second book in the series of knitting with two skeins. I include here a collection of varied head coverings from hoods to snoods to helmet liners, from earflap hats to traditional knit caps. In working on these different shaped pieces you will find some interesting ideas for combining colors, such as picking up a stitch in the row below, slip stitch knitting, and double knitting. You will also discover ways to optimize combinations of two completely different yarns to create extra-special warm headgear.

Each hat will demonstrate a different method for combining yarns. In addition to the designs that I created, I've included pieces from 20 designers whose pieces offer their own unique perspectives.

Here's a sampling: Try Judith Rudnick Kane's Drop Stitch Hooded Scarf, which uses an unraveling method to open up the stitches and maximize the use of two full skeins. Incorporate two colors in a lovely Fair Isle design with Tanya Alpert's Fair Isle Cap. Use the knitting in the stitch below method to create a vertically striped cap in Pam Grushkin's Stria Slouch. Lift the slipped stitches to execute Lynn Wilson's Slip Stitch Hat in two colors. Create an interesting pattern for the band using variegated yarn with the Interlocking Cloche designed by Amy Micallef. Use multidirectional techniques to start a bias hat with a flower, in my Flower Hat. Or create a completely reversible double-knit lace hat using Alasdair Post-Quinn's very unusual and previously unpublished methods for doing this.

These projects are suitable for all levels, from beginner to advanced, and the wide range of techniques offers many opportunities to add new skills to your repertoire. Before you begin, be sure to read through the Techniques chapter, to get a sense of how some of the stitch patterns and techniques are used.

Use what you can from this book, but most important, let the skills you learn here advance your knitting in such a way that you will be able to incorporate them into future projects. Please share your project photos with me, either at www.facebook.com/artyarns or through this book's page on www.ravelry.com. And happy knitting!

Dotson Hat

materials and tools

Artyarns Supermerino (100% superwash merino wool; 1.75oz/50g =
104yd/95m): (A), 1 skein color beige #257—approx 104yd/95m of
medium weight yarn (4)

Artyarns Beaded Silk Light (100% silk with Murano glass beads;
1.75oz/50g = 160yd/146m): (B), 1 skein color gold #257—approx
160yd/146m of lightweight yarn (3)

Knitting needles: 4.5mm (size 7 U.S.) 16"/41cm circular and double
pointed needles or size to obtain gauge

Stitch markers

Tapestry needle

gauge

18 sts/28 rows = 4"/10cm in St st using A

Always take time to check your gauge.

finished measurements

18 (20)"/46 (51)cm circumference

This is a slouchy hat worked
in a simple stitch with a nice
texture that is enhanced
with beads. It starts with a
hemmed brim for sturdiness
and a picot edge for fun.

design by
Jennifer Wood

skill level
easy

pattern stitch

DOT
Rnds 1 and 3: Knit.
Rnd 2: *K1, p1, rep from * around.
Rnd 4: *P1, k1, rep from * around.
Rep rnds 1–4 for pat.

instructions

BRIM
With A, CO 81 (90) sts. PM and join, being careful not to twist the sts. Work in St st for 7 rnds.

Next (picot) rnd: *K1, k2tog, yo, rep from * around. Work in St st for 8 rnds.

Next rnd: Purl, dec 1 (0) st—80 (90) sts.

Join B. With A and B held tog, work in Dot st until piece measures 6¼"/16cm, ending with rnd 4 of pat.

SHAPE CROWN
NOTE: *Change to dpns when needed.*

Next (dec) rnd: *K13 (15), sl 2-k1-p2sso; rep from * around—70 (80) sts.

Work rnd 2 of Dot st.

Next (dec) rnd: *K11 (13), sl 2-k1-p2sso; rep from * around—60 (70) sts.

Work rnd 4 of Dot st.

Continue in this manner, dec every other rnd working 2 less sts in between dec, followed by the appropriate rnd of Dot st, until 20 sts rem.

Next (dec) rnd: *K2tog; rep from * around—10 sts. Cut yarn, draw tail through rem sts and secure.

FINISHING
Fold brim at picot rnd, sew in place on WS. Weave in ends.

Colombina

materials and tools

Artyarns Silk Pearl (100% silk; 1.75oz/50g = 170yd/155m): (A), 1 skein color blue #225—approx 170yd/155m of lightweight yarn

Artyarns Beaded Mohair & Sequins (80% silk, 20% kid mohair with glass beads and sequins; 1.75oz/50g = 114yd/104m): (B), 1 skein color gold #182—approx 114yd/104m of lightweight yarn

Knitting needles: 4mm (size 6 U.S.) 16"/41cm circular and double pointed needles or size to obtain gauge

3.25 (size 3 U.S.) 16"/41cm circular needle

Stitch marker

Tapestry needle

Elastic thread (optional)

gauge

24 sts/26 rows = 4"/10cm in St st using larger needles and A

Always take time to check your gauge.

finished measurements

19"/48cm circumference

A silky slouch hat for all seasons is such a fun knit with sparkles and stripes.

design by
Daniela Johannsenova

skill level
easy

● ● ● ●

pattern stitch

STRIPE

*With A, work 4 rnds; with B, work 2 rnds. Rep from *.

instructions

BRIM

With smaller needles and A, loosely CO 114 sts. PM and join, being careful not to twist the sts. Work in k1, p1 rib for 15 rnds. Change to larger needles.

Next rnd: (K1, yo, k1, sl 2-k1-p2sso, k1, yo) 19 times.

Next rnd: Knit.

Rep last 2 rnds twice more.

Change to B.

Next rnd: (K1, yo, k1, yo, k3tog, yo, k1, yo) 19 times—152 sts.

Next rnd: Knit.

Work in Stripe pat 6 times (36 rnds).

SHAPE CROWN

NOTE: *Change to dpns when needed.*

Change to A.

Next rnd: Knit.

Next (dec) rnd: *K2tog; rep from * around—76 sts.

Next rnd: Knit.

Change to B and knit 2 rnds.

Change to A and knit 2 rnds.

Next (dec) rnd: *K2tog; rep from * around—38 sts.

Change to B and knit 2 rnds.

Change to A.

Knit 2 rnds.

Next (dec) rnd: *K2tog; rep from * around—19 sts.

Change to B and knit 2 rnds.

Change to A.

Knit 1 rnd.

Next (dec) rnd: (K2tog) 9 times, k1—10 sts.

Cut yarn, draw tail through rem sts and secure.

FINISHING

Weave in ends. If needed, weave a length of elastic thread through edge of brim and pull to adjust fit of hat.

Eleganza

materials and tools

Artyarns Ultramerino 8 (100% merino wool; 3.5oz/100g = 188yd/172m): (A), 1 skein color tonal green #2234—approx 188yd/172m of medium weight yarn (4)

Artyarns Beaded Mohair & Sequins (80% silk, 20% kid mohair with glass beads and sequins; 3.5oz/50g = 114yd/104m): (B), 1 skein color gold #246—approx 114yd/104m of lightweight yarn (3)

Knitting needles: 5.5mm (size 9 U.S.) 16"/41cm circular and double pointed needles or size to obtain gauge

4.5mm (size 7 U.S.) 16"/41cm circular needle

Stitch marker

Safety pin

3"/8cm-long piece of feather trim

Tapestry needle

gauge

18 sts/26 rows = 4"/10cm in St st using larger needles and A

Always take time to check your gauge.

finished measurements

18½"/47cm circumference

Accessorize by adding a feather to match the accent yarn used in this design.

design by
Daniela Johannsenova

skill level
easy

instructions

BRIM

With smaller needles and A, loosely
CO 84 sts. PM and join, being
careful not to twist the sts.

Next 2 rnds: With A, *k1, p1; rep from *
around.

Next 2 rnds: With B, *k1, p1; rep from *
around.

Work last 4 rnds a total of 5 times. Cut
B. Change to larger needles.

Next rnd: With A, *k1, p1; rep from *
around.

Next rnd: *K1, M1, k3; rep from *
around—105 sts. Knit 30 rnds.

SHAPE CROWN

NOTE: *Change to dpns when needed.*

Next (dec) rnd: *K2tog; rep from * to
last st, k1—53 sts.

Knit 4 rnds.

Next (dec) rnd: *K2tog; rep from * to
last st, k1—27 sts.

Next rnd: Knit. Cut yarn, draw tail
through rem sts and secure.

FINISHING

Weave in ends.

FEATHER BROOCH

Fold feather trim in half and attach to
hat with a safety pin.

Helmet Liner

materials and tools

Artyarns Supermerino (100% superwash merino wool; 3.5oz/100g = 208 yd/190m): (A), 1 skein color burgundy #300—approx 208yd/190m of medium weight yarn (4)

Artyarns Cashmere 3 (100% cashmere; 1.75oz/50g = 170yd/155m): (B), 1 skein color maroon variegated #161—approx 170yd/155m of fine weight yarn (2)

Knitting needles: 5mm (size 8 U.S.) 16"/41cm circular needle or size to obtain gauge

Stitch markers

Tapestry needle

gauge

12 sts/16 rows = 4"/10cm in St st with A and B held tog

Always take time to check your gauge.

finished measurements

14"/36cm circumference x 15"/38cm long

This is a cowl and hood in one. Knitted in one piece from bottom to top, this versatile piece will be sure to keep you toasty warm.

design by
Iris Schreier

skill level
easy

instructions

Note: Both yarns A and B are held together throughout.

COWL

With both yarns held tog, CO 40 sts. PM and join, being careful not to twist the sts.

Rnd 1: Knit.

Rnd 2: Purl.

Rnds 3–6: Rep rnds 1 and 2.

Rnds 7–14: Knit.

Rnds 15–20: (K1, p1) 6 times, knit to end.

Rnd 21: BO 13 sts, k13, PM, M1L, k1, M1R, PM, k13—2 sts inc.

HOOD

NOTE: *Work back and forth in rows.*

Row 1 (WS): K3, purl to last 3 sts, k3.

Row 2: Knit to marker, sm, M1L, knit to marker, M1R, sm, knit to end—2 sts inc.

Rep rows 1 and 2 until there are 67 sts, ending with a WS row.

Next row (RS): Knit.

Next row: K3, purl to last 3 sts, k3.

Rep last 2 rows a total of 4 times.

FINISHING

With WS facing, fold top edge in half and join with three-needle bind-off (page 118). Weave in ends.

Drop Stitch Hooded Scarf

This elegant hooded scarf drapes beautifully. The dropped stitches create a warm, open, lacy effect.

design by
Judith Rudnick Kane

skill level
easy

materials and tools

Artyarns Cashmere Sock Yarn (67% cashmere, 25% wool, 8% nylon; 1.75oz/50g = 160 yd/146m): (A), 1 skein color pale blue variegated #1007; (B) 1 skein color pale olive tonal #2296—approx 320yd/192m of fine weight yarn (2)

Knitting needles: 3.5mm (size 4 U.S.) or size to obtain gauge

Tapestry needle

gauge

20 sts/40 rows = 4"/10cm in pat

Always take time to check your gauge.

finished measurements

7½" x 63"/19cm x 160cm, after dropping sts and before seaming

instructions

With A, CO 35 sts.

Row 1: *K3, p1; rep from * to last 3 sts, k3.

Rep row 1, alternating A and B every 2 rows until piece measures 63"/160cm.

Next row: K3, *drop next st, kfb, k2; rep from * across. BO loosely in pat.

FINISHING

Unravel all dropped sts to the CO row. Fold scarf in half lengthwise. With tapestry needle, seam back of hood 11"/28cm, starting at fold. Weave in ends.

Drawstring Hat with a Little Splash

materials and tools

Artyarns Silk Rhapsody (50% silk, 50% kid mohair; 3.5oz/100g = 260yd/238m): (A), 1 skein color pale peach brown #H10—approx 260yd/238m of medium weight yarn (4)

Artyarns Mohair Splash (74% silk, 26% kid mohair with Murano glass beads and sequins; 1.75oz/50g = 165yd/151m): (B), 1 skein color gold #H10—approx 165yd/151m of lightweight yarn (3)

Knitting needles: U.S. size 8 (5mm) 16"/41cm circular and double pointed needles or size to obtain gauge

U.S. size 7 (4.5mm) 16"/41cm circular needle

Stitch marker

Tapestry needle

gauge

22 sts/28 rows = 4"/10cm in Lace pat using larger needles and A

Always take time to check your gauge.

finished measurements

20"/51cm circumference x 14"/36cm long

This is a fun hat to be worn day or night, with a touch of sequins and beads. It can be worn as a hat by tying the top, or as a neck warmer or a snood when untied.

design by
Sharon Sorken

skill level
intermediate

pattern stitch

LACE

Rnd 1: *K3, k3tog tbl, k3, yo, k1, yo; rep from * around.

Rnd 2 and all even rnds: Knit.

Rnd 3: *K2, k3tog tbl, k2, yo, k3, yo; rep from * around.

Rnd 5: *K1, k3tog tbl, k1, yo, k5, yo; rep from * around.

Rnd 7: *K3tog tbl, yo, k7, yo; rep from * around.

Rnd 9: *Yo, k1, yo, k3, k3tog tbl, k3; rep from * around.

Rnd 11: *Yo, k3, yo, k2, k3tog tbl, k2; rep from * around.

Rnd 13: *Yo, k5, yo, k1, k3tog tbl, k1; rep from * around.

Rnd 15: *Yo, k7, yo, k3tog tbl; rep from * around.

Rnd 16: Knit.

Rep rnds 1–16 for pat.

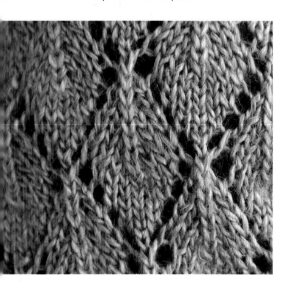

pattern chart

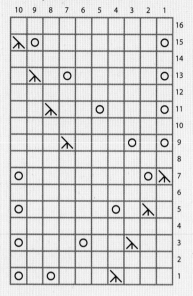

☐ knit

⋏ k3tog through back loop

○ yo

instructions

BRIM

With smaller needles and B, CO 108 sts. PM and join, being careful not to twist the sts. Work in k2, p2 rib for 2"/5cm. Change to larger needles and A.

Next rnd: Knit, inc 2 sts evenly—110 sts.

Change to Lace pat and work even until piece measures 9"/23cm from beg. On last rnd, dec 2 sts evenly—108 sts. Change to smaller needles and B. Work in k2, p2 rib for 2"/5cm. BO in pat.

FINISHING

TIE

With smaller needles and A, CO 3 sts. Work in I-cord (page 124) for 34"/86cm. Bind off.

Weave in ends. Block. Thread I-cord through the last row and pull to gather.

Scalloped Feather and Fan Hat

The feather and fan pattern at the bottom of this hat makes a nice, decorative border and allows the knitter to try out a quick and easy lace pattern.

design by
Sinje Ollen

skill level
easy

materials and tools

Artyarns Cottonspring (100% cotton; 1.75oz/50g = 165yd/151m): (A), 1 skein color pink #2295; (B), 1 skein color pink #163—approx 330yd/302m of lightweight yarn (3)

Knitting needles: 3.5mm (size 4 U.S.) 16"/41cm circular and double pointed needles or size to obtain gauge

Stitch markers

Tapestry needle

gauge

20 sts/34 rows = 4"(10cm) in St st

Always take time to check your gauge.

finished measurements

19"/48cm circumference

pattern stitch

FEATHER AND FAN

Rnd 1: With A, purl.

Rnd 2: *(K2tog) 3 times, (k1, yo) 6 times, (k2tog) 3 times; rep from * around.

Rnds 3 and 4: With A, knit.

instructions

BRIM

With A, CO 144 sts. Work in Feather and Fan pat for 12 rnds.

Rnd 13: With A, purl.

Rnd 14: (K2tog) 3 times, k6, (k2tog) 3 times; rep from * around—96 sts.

Rnd 15: With A, knit.

Rnd 16: With A, purl.

Rnds 17 and 18: With A, knit.

Rnd 19: With B, knit.

Rnd 20: With B, purl.

Rnds 21–23: With A, knit.

Rnd 24: With A, purl.

Rnd 25: With B, knit. Work even in B until piece measures 6"/15cm. PM every 24 sts.

SHAPE CROWN

NOTE: *Change to dpns when needed.*

Next (dec) rnd: *K2tog, knit to 2 sts before next marker, k2tog; rep from * around—8 sts dec. Maintaining stripe pat, rep dec rnd every other rnd until 8 sts rem. Rep dec rnd every rnd until 4 sts rem. Cut yarn, draw tail through rem sts and secure.

FINISHING

Weave in ends. Block.

Swirl Hat

materials and tools

Artyarns Cashmere Glitter: (100% cashmere with Lurex; 1.75oz/50g = 170yd/155m): (A), 1 skein color camel #321—approx 170yd/155m of fine weight yarn

Artyarns Mohair Splash (74% silk, 26% kid mohair with Murano glass beads and sequins; 1.75oz/50g = 165yd/151m): (B), 1 skein color camel #321—approx 165yd/151m of lightweight yarn

Knitting needles: 3.75mm (size 5 U.S.) 24"/61cm circular needle or size to obtain gauge

3.25mm (size 3 U.S.) 16"/41cm circular needle

Waste yarn

Stitch marker

Tapestry needle

gauge

19 sts/30 rows = 4"/10cm in Swirl Lace pat using larger needles and A and B held tog

Always take time to check your gauge.

special abbreviation

skp: slip 1 st knitwise with yarn in back, knit next st, pass slipped st over knit st, a dec of 1 st

finished measurements

15 (16)"/38 (41)cm circumference (unstretched)

You will feel as if you are wearing a jeweled crown with this lovely swirl hat. In gold as shown, the hat is a beauty, but just imagine it in ruby red, emerald green, or a silver-gray accent on a blustery winter day! This pattern is quite simple to follow, and the materials are luscious to work with.

design by
Lisa Hoffman

skill level
intermediate

pattern stitch

SWIRL LACE
Rnd 1: *K1, yo, k1, p1, k1, skp; rep from * around.

Rnd 2: Knit.

Rep rnds 1 and 2 for pat.

instructions

BRIM
With smaller needle and A, CO 48 (51) sts using the tubular method (page 116)—96 (102) sts. PM and join, being careful not to twist the sts. Work in k1, p1 rib for 8 rnds. Change to larger needle. Holding A and B tog, work in Swirl Lace pat until piece measures 7½"/19cm from beg, ending with rnd 2.

SHAPE CROWN
Rnd 1: *K2, p1, k1, skp; rep from * around—80 (85) sts.

Rnd 2: Knit.

Rnd 3: *K1, p1, k1, skp; rep from * around—64 (68) sts.

Rnd 4: Knit. Cut yarn, draw tail through rem sts and secure.

FINISHING
Weave in ends. Block lightly.

Lace Beret

materials and tools

Artyarns Cashmere Sock (67% cashmere, 25% wool, 8% nylon; 1.75oz/50g= 160yd/146m): (A), 1 skein color pink and brown variegated #130—approx 160yd/146m of fine weight yarn

Artyarns Cashmere Glitter (100% cashmere with metallic strand; 1.75oz/50g = 170yd/155m): (B), 1 skein color silver #130—approx 170yd/155m of fine weight yarn

Knitting needles: 3.75mm (size 5 U.S.) 16"/41cm circular and double pointed needles or size to obtain gauge

3.25mm (size 3 U.S.) 16"/41cm circular needle

Waste yarn

Stitch markers

Tapestry needle

gauge

20 sts/28 rows = 4"/10cm in St st using larger needles and B

Always take time to check your gauge.

finished measurements

19"/48cm circumference

This openwork tam is sporty and elegant, perfect for all occasions.

design by
Brooke Nico

skill level
intermediate

pattern chart

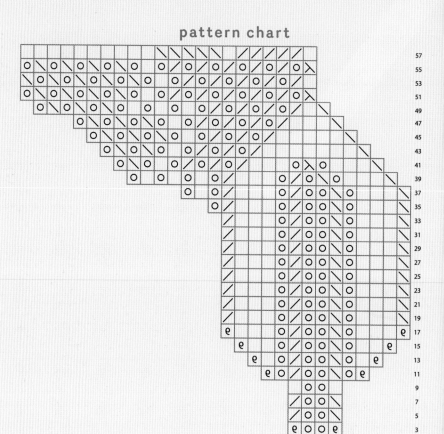

e	knit through the back loop
☐	knit
⧄	slip 1, k2tog, psso
╱	k2tog
╲	ssk
O	yo
V	knit front and back

instructions

NOTE: Hat is knit from the top down. An umbilical cord cast on in waste yarn is an easy way to start with such a small circle.

CROWN

With larger needle and waste yarn, CO 8 sts. Work in St st for 3"/8cm, ending with a WS row. Join B, leaving a 6"/15cm tail. With dpns, place 2 sts on needle 1 and 3 sts on each of needles 2 and 3. Join, being careful not to twist the sts.

Beg chart, noting the even rnds are not charted and are all knit. Pay particular attention to special instructions on rnds 54 and 55. Work chart through rnd 57.

BRIM

Join A. Work in St st for 12 rnds. Change to smaller needle and work in k2, p1 rib for 8 rnds. BO loosely in pat.

FINISHING

Remove waste yarn, and place resulting 8 sts on dpns. Draw tail through rem sts and secure. Weave in ends. Block.

Silk Cloche

materials and tools

Artyarns Silk Pearl (100% silk; 1.75oz/50g = 170yd/155m): (A), 1 skein
color pale blue #246—approx 170yd/155m of lightweight yarn

Artyarns Beaded Pearl (100% silk with glass beads; 1.75 oz/50g =
100yd/91m): (B), 1 skein pale blue #246G—approx 100yd/91m of
medium weight yarn

Knitting needles: 3.5mm (size 4 U.S.) 16"/41cm circular and double
pointed needles or size to obtain gauge

Stitch marker

Tapestry needle

gauge

21 sts and 26 rows = 4"/10cm in Lace pat using A

Always take time to check your gauge.

finished measurements

16 (17)"/41 (43)cm circumference

Combine pale blue with golden beads in this dressy and elegant "flapper" or cloche style. To give it a bit more current look, Laurie added a very subtle slouch to the body of the hat. The hat is meant to be worn purl side out—with the bands of purl stitches framing the beaded pattern.

design by
Laurie Kimmelstiel

skill level
intermediate

pattern stitches

EYELET

Rnd 1: With B, knit.

Rnd 2: With B, *k2tog, yo; rep from * around.

Rnd 3: With B, knit.

LACE

Rnds 1-5: With A, purl.

Rnds 6-8: With B, work rnds 1-3 of eyelet pat.

Rep rnds 1-8 for pat.

instructions

BRIM

With A, CO 84 (90) sts. PM and join, being careful not to twist the sts. Work in k2, p2 rib for 2 rnds.

Rnds 1-5: Purl.

Rnds 6-10: Knit.

Rnds 11-14: Purl.

Next rnd: *P14 (15), M1p; rep from * around—90 (96) sts.

Work Eyelet pat over next 3 rnds, then work Lace pat 5 times.

With A, purl 5 rnds.

Next rnd: With A, *p13 (14), p2tog; rep from * around—84 (90) sts.

Knit 3 rnds.

SHAPE CROWN

NOTE: *Change to dpns when needed.*

Next rnd: *K4, k2tog; rep from *
around—70 (75) sts.

Next rnd:

Smaller hat: K3, k2tog, knit to last 2
sts, k2tog—68 sts.

Larger hat: K3, k2tog, k3, k2tog, knit
to last 2 sts, k2tog—72 sts.

Knit 2 rnds.

Next rnd: *K2, k2tog; rep from *
around—51 (54) sts.

Knit 3 rnds. Cont shaping as follows:

Rnd 1: *K1 k2tog; rep from *
around—34 (36) sts.

Rnd 2: Knit.

Rnd 3: *K2tog; rep from * around—17
(18) sts.

Next rnd:

Smaller hat: *K2tog; rep from * to last
st, k1—9 sts.

Larger hat: *K2tog; rep from *
around—9 sts.

Cut yarn, draw tail through rem sts
and secure.

FINISHING

Weave in ends. Block lightly.

Lace Snood

Melissa says, "My hands long for the feel of silk and cashmere and my eyes lust after this luscious colorway that reminds me of the vibrant hues of lupines in summer, with the hint of glimmer." Wear it over the head as a snood or as a cowl.

design by
Melissa Morgan Oakes

skill level
intermediate

materials and tools

Artyarns Ensemble Glitter (75% silk, 25% cashmere with Lurex; 3.5oz/100g = 256yd/234m): 2 skeins color bright purple #H5—approx 512yd/468m of medium weight yarn (4)

Knitting needles: 3.5mm (size 4 U.S.) 18"/46cm circular needle or size to obtain gauge

Stitch marker

Tapestry needle

gauge

18 sts/20½ rows = 4"/10cm in pat

Always take time to check your gauge.

finished measurements

27"/69cm circumference x 20½"/52cm long

pattern chart

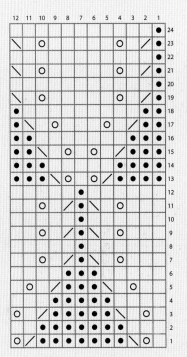

knit • purl
◯ yo ╱ k2tog
╲ ssk

instructions

SNOOD

Loosely CO 120 sts. PM and join, being careful not to twist the sts. Work in garter st for 3 rnds, beg with a purl rnd (purl 1 rnd, knit 1 rnd, purl 1 rnd). Beg chart, work until piece measures approx 20"/51cm long. Work in garter st for 3 rnds as before. BO loosely.

FINISHING

Weave in ends. Block.

Slip Stitch Hat

materials and tools

Artyarns Beaded Cashmere (65% silk, 35% cashmere with glass beads and sequins; 1.75oz/50g = 115yd/105m): (A),1 skein color metal #159—approx 115yd/105m of medium weight yarn

Artyarns Silk Rhapsody (50% silk, 50% kid mohair; 3.5oz/100g = 260yd/238m): (B), 1 skein color cream #250—approx 260yd/238m of medium weight yarn

Knitting needles: 4.5mm (size 7 U.S.) 16"/41cm circular and double pointed needles or size to obtain gauge

4mm (size 6 U.S.) 16"/41cm circular needle

Stitch marker

Yarn needle

gauge

18 sts/24 rows = 4"/10cm in St st using larger needles and B

Always take time to check your gauge.

special abbreviation

KUS: Insert right needle under the loose strand 5 rnds below and knit the next st, bringing the st out under the strand.

finished measurements

18½"/47cm circumference

This beautiful hat is knit seamlessly in the round. The brim is knit using a mock ribbing pattern that helps the luxurious cashmere keep its shape. The top of the hat is knit using a beautiful slip stitch pattern that looks complicated but is surprisingly easy to knit.

design by
Lynn M. Wilson

skill level
intermediate
● ● ● ●

pattern stitch

SLIP STITCH

Rnd 1: With A, *K3, sl 3 wyif; rep from * around.

Rnds 2, 3, 4, 5: With B, knit.

Rnd 6: With A, *sl 3 wyib, k1, KUS, k1; rep from * around.

Rnd 7: With A, *sl 3 wyif, k3; rep from * around.

Rnds 8, 9, 10, 11: With B, knit.

Rnd 12: With A, *k1, KUS, k1, sl 3 wyib; rep from * around.

Rep rnds 1–12 for pat.

instructions

BRIM

With smaller needle and A, CO 99 sts. PM and join, being careful not to twist the sts.

Rnd 1: *P1, sl 2 wyib; rep from * around.

Rnd 2: Knit.

Rep rnds 1 and 2 a total of 7 times, then work rnd 1 once more. Change to larger needle.

Next rnd: [(K2tog; k4) 3 times, k2tog, k7] 3 times; (k2tog, k4) 3 times— 84 sts.

With B, knit 1 rnd.

Next rnd: With A, *k3, sl 3 wyib; rep from * around.

Work rnds 1–12 of Slip Stitch pat 3 times, then work rnds 1–7 once more.

SHAPE CROWN

NOTE: *Change to dpns when needed.*

Rnd 1: With B, *k4, ssk; rep from * around—70 sts.

Rnds 2, 4: With B, knit.

Rnd 3: With B, *k3, ssk; rep from * around—56 sts.

Rnd 5: With A, k1, *KUS, k3; rep from * to last 3 sts, KUS, k2.

Rnd 6: With A, k1, *ssk, k2; rep from * to last 3 sts, ssk, k1—42 sts.

Rnd 7: With B, k1, *sl 1 wyib, k2; rep from * to last 2 sts, sl 1 wyib, k1.

Rnd 8: With B, k1, *sl 1 wyib, ssk; rep from * to last 2 sts, sl 1 wyib, ssk last st with first st of the rnd; replace marker after the ssk—28 sts.

Rnd 9: With A, *k1, sl1 wyib; rep from * around.

Rnd 10: With A, *ssk; rep from * around—14 sts.

Rnd 11: With A, knit.

Rnd 12: With A, *ssk; rep from * around—7 sts. Cut yarn, draw tail through rem sts and secure.

FINISHING

Weave in ends. Block.

Soft Cloche

materials and tools

Artyarns Cashmere 1 (100% cashmere; 1.75oz/50g = 510yd/466m):
(A), 1 skein color light grey #272—approx 510yd/466m of lace weight
yarn

Artyarns Beaded Ensemble (80% silk, 20% cashmere; 3.5oz/100g=
167yd/153m): (B), 1 skein color medium gray w/ silver beads
#247—approx 167yd/153m of medium weight yarn

Knitting needles: 4.5mm (size 7 U.S.) 16"/41cm circular and double
pointed needles or size to obtain gauge

Stitch markers

Tapestry needle

½ yd/0.5m organza ribbon, ¼"/0.5cm wide

gauge

20 sts/22 rows = 4"/10cm in pat using B

Always take time to check your gauge.

special abbreviations

sl 1 : Slip 1 st knitwise with yarn in back

sl2tog-p1-p2sso: Slip 2 sts tog knitwise, p 1 st, pass 2 sl sts over the p st, a
dec of 2 sts

finished measurements

20"/51cm circumference

This feminine and graceful
piece evokes the styles of
long ago, yet has that modern
sophistication that enhances
any wardrobe.

design by
Laura Zukaite

skill level
intermediate

instructions

BRIM

With A, CO 200 sts. PM and join, being
  careful not to twist the sts. Work in
  k1, p1 rib for ½"/1cm.

Next (dec) rnd: *P2tog, k2tog; rep
  from * around—100 sts. Work in k1,
  p1 rib for 2 rnds.

Next (eyelet) rnd: *K2tog, yo, (p1, k1)
  4 times; rep from * around. Work in
  k1, p1 rib for 1½"/4cm more. Change
  to B.

Rnd 1: *P4, sl 1 knitwise, p5; rep
  from * around.

Rnd 2: *P4, k1, p5; rep from * around.

Rep last 2 rnds for 3½"/9cm, ending
  with rnd 2.

SHAPE CROWN

NOTE: *Change to dpns when needed.*

Next (dec) rnd: *P3, sl2tog-p1-p2sso,
  p4; rep from * around—80 sts.

Work even in pat for 5 rnds.

Next (dec) rnd: *P2, sl2tog-p1-p2sso,
  p3; rep from * around—60 sts.

Work even in pat for 5 rnds.

Next (dec) rnd: *P1, sl2tog-p1-p2sso,
  p2; rep from * around—40 sts.

Work even in pat for 5 rnds.

Next (dec) rnd: *Sl2tog-p1-p2sso, p1;
  rep from * around—20 sts.

Work even in pat for 1 rnd. Move
  marker 1 st forward.

Next (dec) rnd: *K2tog; rep from *
  around—10 sts. Cut yarn, draw
  through rem sts and secure.

FINISHING

Weave in ends. Block. Weave ribbon
  through the eyelets and tie in a bow.

Ear Flap Hat

materials and tools

Artyarns Ultramerino 8 (100% merino wool; 3.5oz/100g = 188yd/172m): (A), 1 skein color black #246; (B), 1 skein color pink/orange multi #190—approx 376yd/344m of medium weight yarn

Knitting Needles: 4.5mm (size 7 U.S.) 16"/41cm circular and double pointed needles or size to obtain gauge

3.75mm (size F U.S.) crochet hook

Stitch holders

Stitch markers

Waste yarn

Tapestry needle

gauge

18 sts/36 rows = 4"/10cm in garter st

Always take time to check your gauge.

finished measurements

18"/46cm circumference

This fun hat design combines garter stitch with an easy-to-knit slip stitch pattern. Change the look completely by using less contrasting yarns. This hat can easily be made for a teen or older child by using needles that are one size smaller than those described in these instructions.

design by
Lynn M. Wilson

skill level
intermediate

instructions

EAR FLAPS (MAKE 2)

With A, CO 3 sts. Work as follows, joining B as directed and carrying color not in use loosely up the side of the work.

Rows 1, 4, 5, 8, 9, 12, 13, 16, 17, 20, 21, 24, 25, 28, 29, 32, 33, 36, 37: With A, knit.

Row 2 (RS): With B, k1, M1, k1, M1, k1—5 sts.

Rows 3, 7, 11, 15, 19, 23, 27, 30, 31, 34, 35, 38, 39: With B, knit.

Rows 6, 10, 14, 18, 22, 26: With B, k1, M1, knit across to last st, M1, k1—2 sts inc, ending with 17 sts. Cut yarn, place sts on holder.

BRIM

With A, CO 9 sts using Cable or Knitted method (page 114), knit across earflap, CO 28 sts, knit across 2nd earflap, CO 9 sts—80 sts. PM and join, being careful not to twist the sts.

Rnds 1 and 5: With A, purl.

Rnds 2 and 6: With B, knit.

Rnds 3 and 7: With B, purl.

Rnds 4 and 8: With A, knit.

Next rnd: With A, *k7, kfb; rep from * around—90 sts.

Rnd 1: With B, k3, *sl 1, k5; rep from * to last 3 sts, sl 1, k2.

Rnd 2: With B, p3, *sl 1, p5; rep from * to last 3 sts, sl 1, p2.

Rnd 3: With A, *sl 1, k5; rep from * around.

Rnd 4: With A, *sl 1, p5; rep from * around.

Rnd 5: With B, k1, sl 1; *k5, sl 1; rep from * to last 4 sts, k4.

Rnd 6: With B, p1, sl 1; *p5, sl 1; rep from * to last 4 sts, p4.

Rnd 7: With A, k4, *sl 1, k5; rep from * to last 2 sts, sl 1, k1.

Rnd 8: With A, p4, *sl 1, p5; rep from * to last 2 sts, sl 1, p1.

Rnd 9: With B, *k5, sl 1; rep from * around.

Rnd 10: With B, *p5, sl 1; rep from * around.

Rnd 11: With A, k2; *sl 1, k5; rep from * to last 4 sts, sl 1, k3.

Rnd 12: With A, p2; *sl 1, p5; rep from * to last 4 sts, sl 1, p3.

Rnds 13-36: Repeat rnds 1-12 two times

Rnds 37-44: Repeat rnds 1-8 one time

SHAPE CROWN

NOTE: *Change to dpns when needed.*

Rnd 1: With B, *k2tog, k3, sl 1; rep from * around—75 sts.

Rnd 2: With B, *p4, sl 1; rep from * around.

Rnd 3: With A, k1, sl 1, *k4, sl 1; rep from * to last 3 sts, k3.

Rnd 4: With A, p1, sl 1; *p4, sl 1; rep from * to last 3 sts, p3.

Rnd 5: With B, *k2, sl 1, k2tog; rep from * around—60 sts.

Rnd 6: With B, p2, sl 1; *p3, sl 1; rep from * to last st, p1.

Rnd 7: With A, *sl 1, k3; rep from * around.

Rnd 8: With A, *sl 1, p3; rep from * around.

Rnd 9: With B, *k1, sl 1, k2tog; rep from * around—45 sts.

Rnd 10: With B, p1, sl 1; *p2, sl 1; rep from * to last st, p1.

Rnd 11: With A, knit.

Rnd 12: With A, purl.

Rnd 13: With B, *k3, k2tog; rep from * around—36 sts.

Rnd 14: With B, purl.

Rnd 15: With A, *k2, k2tog; rep from * around—27 sts.

Rnd 16: With A: purl.

Rnd 17: With B, *k1, k2tog; rep from * around—18 sts.

Rnd 18: With B, purl.

Rnd 19: With A, *k2tog; rep from * around—9 sts.

Rnd 20: With A, purl.

Cut yarn, draw tail through rem sts and secure.

FINISHING

Weave in ends.

With crochet hook and A, work 1 row of single crochet around each ear flap. Fasten off.

TWISTED CORD TIES (MAKE 2)

Cut ten 20"/51cm lengths each of A and B. Cut one 10"/25cm length of A and two 6"/15cm lengths of waste yarn. Tie bundle of 20"/51cm lengths tog at each end using waste yarn.

Holding one end, twist the opposite end until the cord starts to double back on itself. The more you twist the cord, the tighter the cord will be. Once cord is twisted enough, fold it in half and use the rem length of A to tie both ends securely together. The cord will twist around itself; even out the twists if needed. Remove scrap yarn ties and trim the ends evenly. With A, sew cord to point of ear flap. Rep on opposite ear flap.

Block.

Stria Slouch

materials and tools

Artyarns Ultrabulky (100% merino wool; 3.5oz/100g = 110yd/101m): (A), 1 skein color charcoal #264; (B), 1 skein color pale purple/green/blue variegated #193—approx 220yd/202m of bulky weight yarn

Knitting needles: 5mm (size 8 U.S) needles, either double pointed, two 24"/61cm circular needles, or one 40"/100cm circular needle or size to obtain gauge

4.5mm (size 7 U.S.) needles in same length/type as above

Spare needle one size larger than needles used to obtain gauge

Waste yarn

Locking stitch markers, different colors

4.5mm (size G U.S.) crochet hook (optional)

Tapestry needle

gauge
15 sts/17 rows = 4"/10cm in K1b Column pat using larger needles and A

Always take time to check your gauge.

special abbreviation
K1b (knit 1 below): Insert needle into center of st below st on needle, knit as usual, and let st on needle drop.

finished measurements
approx 18 (20)"/46 (51)cm circumference

The knit-one-below technique works beautifully with two shades of yarn, one semisolid and one variegated. It shows off the color play to its best advantage. Knitting a garter brim creates an interesting contrast with the rest of the hat, while continuing the play on colors.

design by
Pam Grushkin

skill level
intermediate

pattern stitch

K1B COLUMN

Note: Always twist yarns at beg of rnd to avoid holes.

Rnd 1: With A, *k1, k1b; rep from * around.

Rnd 2: With B, *k1b, k1; rep from * around.

Rep rnds 1 and 2 for pat.

instructions

BRIM

With smaller needles and A, CO 14 sts using Long Tail Provisional CO (page 115). Cut waste yarn. Knit next row. Join B.

Row 1: Knit.

Row 2: Sl 1 st pwise wyif, bring yarn to back, knit to end.

Rep last 2 rows, alternating 2 rows of A and 2 rows of B, until there are 56 (60) garter ridges. Work 1 more row in A. Cut yarn, leaving a 20"/51cm tail. Remove provisional CO and place sts on needle. With B, join ends using a three-needle bind-off (page 118), purling all sts. Turn seam to WS.

With larger needles and B, pick up and knit 1 st in each sl st along edge. PM and join. Knit 1 rnd, inc evenly to 72 (80) sts. Join A and work in K1b Column pat until piece measures 8½ (9 ½)"/22 (24)cm from beg, ending with rnd 2 and B.

SHAPE CROWN

NOTE: *Change to dpns when needed.*

Next (dec) rnd: With A, *k6 (7), sl 2-k1-p2sso; rep from * around. Mark dec sts with locking st markers. Mark last dec st with a different colored marker for end of rnd—56 (64) sts.

Maintain K1b Column pat throughout, taking note of the modification in rnd 1.

Rnd 1: With B, work rnd 2 of K1b Column pat, knit the marked st regardless of pat. Move marker up with each rnd completed.

Rnd 2: With A, work rnd 1 of K1b Column pat.

Rnd 3: With B, work rnd 2 of K1b Column pat.

Rnd 4: With A, work rnd 1 of K1b Column pat.

Rnd 5: With B, work rnd 2 of K1b Column pat.

Next (dec) rnd: *With A, work to 1 st before marked st, sl 2-k1-p2sso; rep from * around—16 sts dec. Note: Because of the nature of the double dec, the last dec uses the 1st st of the next rnd. This means subsequent rnds may beg with the 2nd st in the K1b Column pat; take care to keep pat aligned as work progresses. Rep from ** until 8 (16) sts rem.

Next rnd (larger size only): *Ssk; rep from * around—8 sts. Cut yarn, draw through rem sts and secure.

FINISHING

With crochet hook and A, work 1 rnd of single crochet around lower edge, fasten off. Weave in ends. Block.

Colorwork Toque

materials and tools

Artyarns Silk Pearl (100% silk; 1.75oz/50g = 170yd/155m): (A), 1 skein color midnight blue #303—approx 170yd/155m of lightweight yarn [3]

Artyarns Beaded Pearl (100% silk with glass beads; 1.75oz/50g = 100yd/91m): (B), 1 skein color harvest #1018—approx 100yd/91m of medium weight yarn [4]

Knitting needles: 4mm (size 6 U.S.) 16"/41cm circular and double pointed needles or size to obtain gauge

Waste yarn

Crochet hook

6 (8, 10, 12) stitch markers

Tapestry needle

gauge

20 sts/28 rows = 4"/10cm in St st

Always take time to check your gauge.

finished measurements

14½ (19¼, 24, 28¾)"/37 (49, 61, 73)cm circumference

This pillbox-style hat is so sophisticated and well crafted that you can barely tell it is handmade. An unusual design that will never go out of style.

design by
Annie Modesitt

skill level
intermediate

colorwork brim chart

BRIM

With waste yarn and A, CO 72 (96, 120, 144) sts using crochet provisional CO (see page 115). PM and join, being careful not to twist the sts. Work in garter st for 4 rnds, then change to B and work in garter st for 2 rnds. Work in Colorwork Brim chart until piece measures 4 (4½, 5, 5½)"/10 (12, 13, 14)cm from beg. With A, knit 1 rnd, then with B, work in garter st for 2 rnds, PM every 12 sts for a total of 6 (8, 10, 12) markers.

SHAPE CROWN

NOTE: *Change to dpns when needed.*

Next rnd: With A, knit.

Next rnd: *Ssk, knit to next marker; rep from * around—6 (8, 10, 12) sts dec. Rep last 2 rnds until 6 (8, 10, 12) sts rem.

Next rnd: *Ssk, rep from * around— 3 (4, 5, 6) sts. Cut yarn, draw tail through rem sts and secure.

FINISHING
EDGING

Undo crochet chain and place CO sts on needles. With B, work I-cord BO (page 118). Graft ends tog. With RS facing, pick up and knit 72 (96, 120, 144) sts around upper edge of colorwork section, on purl rnd before start of crown shaping. With B, work I-cord BO as before.

Weave in ends. Block.

Sun Goddess Chullo

materials and tools

Artyarns Ultramerino 8 (100% merino wool; 3.5oz/ 100g = 188yd/171m): (A), 1 skein color teal #227; (B), 1 skein color sungold #201—approx 376yd/342m of medium weight yarn

Knitting needles: 4.5mm (size 7 U.S.) 16"/41cm circular and double pointed needles or size to obtain gauge

Stitch marker

Tapestry needle

Stitch holder

Crochet hook 5.5mm (size I-9 U.S.)

gauge

20 sts/24 rows = 4"/10cm in Fair Isle pat

Always take time to check your gauge.

finished measurements

20"/51cm circumference

This oversized multipurpose hat will appeal to both women and men alike. Fat ear flaps, long braids, and great color make this chullo a must-knit. Simple charts with easy repeats make this hat ideal for a first-time Fair Isle project.

design by
Lisa Ellis

skill level
intermediate
● ● ● ●

pattern chart 1 Ear Flap

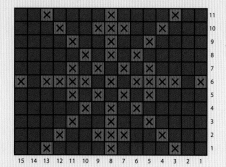

11 10 9 8 7 6 5 4 3 2 1

15 14 13 12 11 10 9 8 7 6 5 4 3 2 1

⊠ color B

■ color A

pattern chart 2

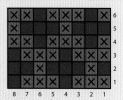

6 5 4 3 2 1

8 7 6 5 4 3 2 1

⊠ color B

■ color A

pattern chart 3

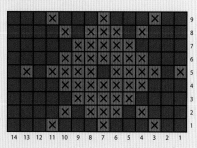

9 8 7 6 5 4 3 2 1

14 13 12 11 10 9 8 7 6 5 4 3 2 1

⊠ color B

■ color A

pattern chart 4

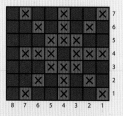

7 6 5 4 3 2 1

8 7 6 5 4 3 2 1

⊠ color B

■ color A

pattern chart 5

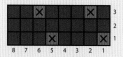

3 2 1

8 7 6 5 4 3 2 1

⊠ color B

■ color A

instructions

EAR FLAPS (MAKE 2)

With A, CO 13 sts. Working in St st, inc 1 st at beg of next 12 rows—25 sts.

Next row (RS): K5, PM, join B and work row 1 of Chart 1, PM, k5.

Next row: P5, work row 2 of Chart 1, p5. Cont as set until all rows of chart are worked. Cut B. With A, work in St st for 7 rows, ending with a WS row. Place on holder.

BRIM

With A, knit across ear flap, CO 25 sts, knit across second ear flap, CO 25 sts—100 sts. PM and join, being careful not to twist the sts. Knit 2 rnds, inc 4 sts on last rnd—104 sts. Work Chart 2 once.

With A, knit 2 rnds, dec 6 sts on last rnd—98 sts. Work Chart 3 once.

With A, knit 2 rnds, dec 2 sts on last rnd—96 sts. Work Chart 2 once.

With A, knit 2 rnds. Work Chart 4 once.

With A, knit 2 rnds. Work Chart 5 once.

SHAPE CROWN

NOTE: *Change to dpns when needed.*

Rnd 1: *K6, k2tog; rep from* around—84 sts.

Rnds 2, 4, 6: Knit.

Rnd 3: *K5, k2tog; rep from* around—72 sts.

Rnd 5: *K4, k2tog; rep from* around—60 sts.

Rnd 7: *K3, k2tog; rep from* around—48 sts.

Rnd 8: *K2, k2tog; rep from* around—36 sts.

Rnd 9: *K1, k2tog; rep from* around—24 sts.

Rnd 10: *K2tog; rep from* around—12 sts. Cut yarn, draw tail through rem sts and secure.

FINISHING

Weave in ends. With crochet hook and B, work 1 rnd of single crochet around lower edge of hat and ear flaps. Fasten off.

FRINGE

Cut 18 strands each of A and B, 30"/76cm long. With crochet hook, pull half the strands through the lower tip of ear flap evenly. Braid tog. Tie end to secure, trim ends. Rep on other ear flap with the other half of the strands.

Cut 4 strands each of A and B, 13"/33cm long. With crochet hook, pull the strands through the top of the hat and tie tog to create a tassel.

Block.

Fair Isle Cap

Knit in two colors of luxurious cashmere, this cozy cap adds a dash of romantic style to any ensemble. Worked in a simple Fair Isle pattern that adds just enough color to make it sophisticated, this cap is fun to knit and wear.

design by
Tanya Alpert

skill level
intermediate

materials and tools

Artyarns Cashmere 2 (100% cashmere; 1.75 oz/50g, 255yds/233m): (A), 1 skein color gray #247; (B), 1 skein color gold #231—approx 510yd/466m of super fine weight yarn (1)

Knitting needles: 3.5mm (size 4 U.S.) 16"/41cm circular needle or size to obtain gauge

3.25mm (size 3 U.S.) 16"/41cm circular needle

2mm (size B U.S.) crochet hook

Stitch marker

Tapestry needle

Scrap of cardboard

gauge

30 sts/36 rows = 4"/10cm in St st using larger needles
Always take time to check your gauge.

finished measurements

19"/48cm circumference

pattern chart

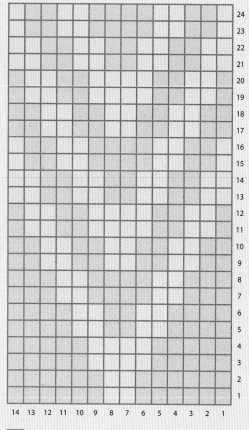

| | | | | | | | | | | | | | | | |
|14|13|12|11|10|9|8|7|6|5|4|3|2|1|

☐ color A

☐ color B

instructions

With smaller needles and A, CO 140 sts. PM and join, being careful not to twist the sts. Work in k2, p2 rib for 2"/5cm. Change to larger needles and work in St st until piece measures 2 ¾"/7cm from beg. Follow chart, working rnds 1–24. With A, work in St st until piece measures 9"/23cm from beg. Change to smaller needles and B. Work in k2, p2 rib for 1"/2.5cm. Bind off in pat.

FINISHING

TIE

With crochet hook and A, work a chain approx 20"/51cm long, leaving tails on each end. Fasten off.

TASSELS (MAKE 2)

Cut a piece of cardboard to approx 2½"/6cm wide. Wrap A around the cardboard 20 times. With a separate piece of yarn, slip under top edge of tassel and tie. Cut opposite ends, wrap another piece of yarn approx ½"/1cm from the top and hide ends in the tassel. Trim. Weave in ends. Block. Lay cap flat and sew tog along BO edge. Thread tie through seam, pull to gather and tie. Sew tassels to ends.

JOINING

Block lightly to size. Join side seam—this seam will become the center back of hat. Join top seam. Pass tie through top corner of both seams and attach tassels. Pull two corners together and tie tassels. Weave in all of the ends.

Chevron Fair Isle Hat

materials and tools

Artyarns Supermerino (100% superwash merino wool; 3.5oz/100g =
208yd/190m): (A), 1 skein, color aqua #2204; (B), 1 skein, color pink/
green/aqua/gray #1006—approx 416yd/380m of medium weight
yarn (4)

Knitting needles: 5mm (size 8 U.S.) 16"/41cm circular and double pointed
needles or size to obtain gauge

4mm (size 6 U.S.) 16"/41cm circular needle

Stitch marker

Tapestry needle

gauge

21 sts/24 rows = 4"/10cm in Colorwork pat using larger needles

Always take time to check your gauge.

finished measurements

22½"/57cm circumference

This slouchy beanie hat is a
fun take on the traditional
style of knitting. By pairing
a solid-colored yarn with a
coordinating variegated, we
get the look of the pattern's
coming and going.

design by
Heather Walpole

skill level
intermediate

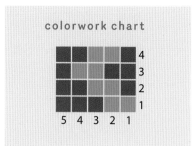

colorwork chart

instructions

BRIM

With smaller needle and A, CO 120 sts. PM and join, being careful not to twist the sts. Work in k2, p2 rib for 1"/2.5cm. Change to larger needles. Join B. Follow Colorwork chart until piece measures 12"/30cm, ending with rnd 4.

SHAPE CROWN

NOTE: *Change to dpns when needed.*

Rnd 1: *With A, k2tog; with B, k3; rep from * around—96 sts.

Rnd 2: *With A, k2tog; with B, k2; rep from * around—72 sts.

Rnd 3: *With A, k2tog; with B, k1; rep from * around—48 sts.

Rnd 4: *With B, k2tog; rep from * around—24 sts.

Rnd 5: *With B, k2tog; rep from * around—12 sts.

Rnd 6: *With B, k2tog; rep from * around—6 sts. Cut yarn, draw tail through rem sts and secure.

FINISHING

Weave in ends. Block.

Cable Headband

materials and tools

Artyarns Cashmere 5 (100% cashmere; 1.75oz/50g = 102yd/93m): (A), 1 skein color purple #240—approx 102yd/93m of medium weight yarn

Artyarns Mohair Splash (74% silk, 26% kid mohair with Murano glass beads and sequins; 1.75oz/50g = 165yd/151m): (B), 1 skein color purple #3273—approx 165yd/151m of lightweight yarn

Knitting needles: 5mm (size 8 U.S.) needles or size to obtain gauge

Cable needle

Tapestry needle

gauge

16 sts/16 rows = 4"/10cm in pat with A and B held tog

Always take time to check your gauge.

special abbreviations

C8B: Sl 4 sts to cable needle and hold in back, k4, k4 from cable needle.

C8F: Sl 4 sts to cable needle and hold in front, k4, k4 from cable needle.

finished measurements

21"/53cm circumference

Whether on the ski slopes or strolling through town, you'll enjoy wearing this elegant headband that warms up the ears yet never interferes with hairstyles.

design by
Iris Schreier

skill level
intermediate

instructions

With A and B held tog, CO 30 sts.

Row 1 (RS): K3, (C8B) 3 times, k3.

Row 2 and all even rows: K3, purl to last 3 sts, k3.

Rows 3 and 5: Knit.

Row 7: K7, (C8F) 2 times, k7.

Rows 9, 11, 13: Knit.

Rep rows 1–14 a total of 6 times. BO.

FINISHING

Sew CO and BO edges tog. Weave in ends.

Broad Street Hat

materials and tools

Artyarns Supermerino (100% superwash merino wool; 1.75oz/50g = 104yd/95m): (A), 1 skein color maroon #256—approx 104yd/95m of medium weight yarn

Artyarns Silk Rhapsody Glitter (50% silk, 50% mohair with Lurex; 3.5oz/100g = 260yd/238m): (B), 1 skein color silver #256—approx 260yd/238m of medium weight yarn

Knitting needles: 6mm (size 10 U.S.) 16"/41cm circular and double pointed needles or size to obtain gauge

Stitch markers

Tapestry needle

gauge

19 sts/24 rows = 4"/10cm in St st with A and B held tog

Always take time to check your gauge.

special abbreviations

C6F: 3 st to front, k3, k3 from cable needle

4lpc: Sl 3 sts to cn, hold to front, p1, k3 from cn

4rpc: Sl 1 st to cn, hold in back, k3, p1 from cn

finished measurements

17½ (19)"/44 (48)cm circumference

This slightly slouchy hat starts with a ribbed brim and moves into rope and diamond cables, which converge like spokes of a wheel. Using the two yarns together gives an exaggerated effect to the cables, while the glitter yarn adds a halo and a nice depth to the cables.

design by
Jennifer Wood

skill level
intermediate

pattern chart 1

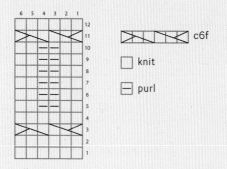

X			c6f
knit			
purl			

pattern chart 2

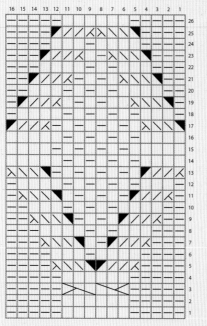

⟍⟍⟍◣	4lpc
◤⟋⟋⟋	4rpc
⟋⟋⟍⟍	c6f
□	knit
⊟	purl

instructions

BRIM

With A and B held tog, CO 84 (92) sts. PM and join, being careful not to twist the sts.

Rnd 1: [(K2, p2) 9 (10) times, k2, p4] 2 times.

Repeat rnd 1 five more times.

Next rnd: *Work rnd 1 of Chart 1, p5 (7), work rnd 1 of Chart 2, p5 (7), work rnd 1 of Chart 1, p4; rep from * around. Cont as set until all 26 rnds of Chart 2 have been worked.

Next rnd: *Work rnd 3 of Chart 1, p10 (12), work rnd 3 of Chart 1, p10 (12), work rnd 3 of Chart 1, p4; rep from * around. Cont as set through rnd 8 of Chart 1.

SHAPE CROWN

NOTE: *Change to dpns when needed.*

Next (dec) rnd: *Work rnd 9 of Chart 1, p2tog-tbl, p6 (8), p2tog, work rnd 9 of Chart 1, p2tog-tbl, p6 (8), p2tog, work rnd 9 of Chart 1, p4; rep from * around—76 (84) sts.

Work 1 rnd even.

Next (dec) rnd: *Work rnd 11 of Chart 1, p2tog-tbl, p4 (6), p2tog, work rnd 11 of Chart 1, p2tog-tbl, p4 (6), p2tog, work rnd 11 of Chart 1, p4; rep from * around—68 (76) sts.

Work 1 rnd even.

Next (dec) rnd: *Work rnd 1 of Chart 1, p2tog-tbl, p2 (4), p2tog, work rnd 1 of Chart 1, p2tog-tbl, p2 (4), p2tog, work rnd 1 of Chart 1, p4; rep from * around—60 (68) sts.

Work 1 rnd even.

Larger size only: *Work rnd 1 of Chart 1, p2tog-tbl, p2, p2tog, work rnd 1 Chart 1, p2tog-tbl, p2, p2tog, work rnd 1 of Chart 1, p4; rep form * around—60 sts.

Next (dec) rnd: *Work rnd 3 of Chart 1, p2, p2tog; rep from * around—54 sts.

Work 1 rnd even.

Next (dec) rnd: *Work rnd 5 of Chart 1, p1, p2tog; rep from * around—48 sts.

Work 1 rnd even.

Next (dec) rnd: *K2, p2tog; rep from * around—36 sts.

Next (dec) rnd: *K1, ssk; rep from * around—24 sts.

Next (dec) rnd: *K2tog; rep from * around—12 sts. Cut yarn, draw tail through rem sts and secure.

FINISHING

Weave in ends.

Bobble Hat

materials and tools

Artyarns Supermerino (100% superwash merino wool; 3.5oz/100g = 208yd/190m): (A), 1 skein color variegated gold/brown/blue/cream #156; (B), 1 skein color solid marigold #231—approx 416yd/380m of medium weight yarn (4)

Knitting needles: 4mm (size 6 U.S.) 16"/41cm circular and double pointed needles or size to obtain gauge

Stitch marker

Tapestry needle

gauge

19 sts/27 rnds =4"/10cm in pat

Always take time to check your gauge.

special abbreviations

MB (make bobble): Knit in the front, back, front, back, and front of next st—5 sts, turn; p5, turn; k5, turn; p2, pass 1st st over 2nd, p3, pass 4th st over last—3 sts; k3tog—1 st.

Garter St in the round: K one round and p next round

finished measurements

18½"/47cm circumference

With a playful topknot and colorful studded bobbles, this unique hat's personality really shines!

design by
Laurie Kimmelstiel

skill level
intermediate

instructions

BRIM

With A, CO 89 sts, pass last st from right needle to left, PM and knit these 2 sts tog, being careful not to twist the sts—88 sts. Work in St st for 2"/5cm. Work in garter st for 8 rnds. Purl next rnd. Knit 10 rnds. Join B.

Next (bobble) rnd: *K7, MB; rep from * around—11 bobbles. With A, knit 10 rnds. Work in garter st for 8 rnds. Purl next rnd.

Next rnd: With B, knit.

Next rnd: With A, knit.

Next rnd: With B, knit.

SHAPE CROWN

NOTE: *Change to dpns when needed. Alternate colors every other rnd as set.*

Rnd 1: *K9, k2tog; rep from * around—80 sts.

Rnd 2: Knit.

Rnd 3: *K8, k2tog; rep from * around—72 sts.

Rnd 4: Knit.

Rnd 5: *K7, k2tog; rep from * around—64 sts.

Rnd 6: *K6, k2tog; rep from * around—56 sts.

Rnd 7: *K5, k2tog; rep from * around—48 sts.

Rnd 8: *K4, k2tog; rep from * around—40 sts.

Rnd 9: *K3, k2tog; rep from * around—32 sts.

Rnd 10: *K2, k2tog; rep from * around—24 sts.

Rnd 11: *K1, k2tog; rep from * around—16 sts.

Rnd 12: *K2tog; rep from * around—8 sts. With A, work in I-cord for 6"/15cm. BO. Tie in overhand knot.

FINISHING

Weave in ends.

Reversible Cable Military Cap

materials and tools

Artyarns Ultramerino 8, (100% merino wool; 3.5oz /100g = 188yd /171m): 2 skeins color navy blue #2267—approx 376yd/342m of medium weight yarn (4)

Knitting needles: 6mm (size 10 U.S.) 16"/41cm circular needle or size to obtain gauge

5mm (size 8 U.S.) 16"/41cm circular and double pointed needles

Waste yarn

Stitch marker

Cable needle

Tapestry needle

gauge

26 sts/24 rows = 4"/10cm in pat using larger needles

Always take time to check your gauge.

special abbreviations

C2R: Sl 1 st to cable needle and hold to back, k1, k1 from cable needle.
C3L: Sl 2 sts to cable needle and hold to front, k1, k2 from cable needle.
C4R: Sl 2 sts to cable needle and hold to back, k2, k2 from cable needle.
C5L: Sl 3 sts to cable needle and hold to front, k2, k3 from cable needle.
C6R: Sl 3 sts to cable needle and hold to back, k3, k3 from cable needle.
C7L: Sl 4 sts to cable needle and hold to front, k3, k4 from cable needle.
C8R: Sl 4 sts to cable needle and hold to back, k4, k4 from cable needle.
C8L: Sl 4 sts to cable needle and hold to front, k4, k4 from cable needle.
RC8R: Sl 4 sts to cable needle and hold to back, k2, p2, k2, p2 from cable needle.
RC8L: Sl 4 sts to cable needle and hold to front, k2, p2, k2, p2 from cable needle.
K2tog-L: Work dec so that sts slant to the left (ssk or k2tog tbl).
K2tog-R: Work dec so that sts slant to the right (k2tog).

finished measurements

17¼ (19¾, 22¼, 24½)"/44 (51, 57, 63)cm circumference

Suitable for any age and gender, this cap is a stylish way to warm the head and shine a spotlight on a gorgeous cable pattern.

design by
Annie Modesitt

skill level
experienced

pattern chart 1
HAT PATTERN

St st
Rev St st
K2tog-L
K2tog-R
C2R
C3L
C4R
C5L
C6R
C7L
C8R
C8L
RC8R
RC8L

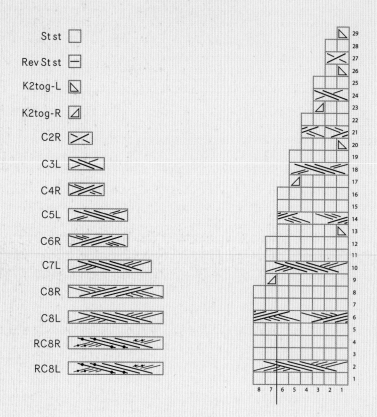

pattern chart 2
REVERSIBLE CABLE FLAP

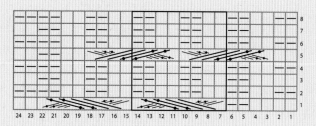

pattern stitches

HAT PATTERN

NOTE: *On rows 6, 14, and 21, the end of the rnd will be past the end of rnd marker; however, keep marker in its same location throughout.*

Rnds 1, 3–5, 7, 8, 11, 12, 15, 16, 19, 22, 25, 28: Knit.

Rnd 2: *C8L; rep from * around.

Rnd 6: K4, *C8R; rep from * around (work last C8R using first 4 sts of rnd).

Rnd 9: *K6, k2tog-R; rep from * around.

Rnd 10: *C7L; rep from * around.

Rnd 13: *K2tog-L, k5; rep from * around.

Rnd 14: K3, *C6R; rep from * around (work last C6R using first 3 sts of rnd).

Rnd 17: *K4, k2tog-R; rep from * around.

Rnd 18: *C5L; rep from * around.

Rnd 20: *K2tog-L, k3; rep from * around.

Row 21: K2, *C4R; rep from * around (work last C4R using first 2 sts of rnd).

Row 23: *K2, k2tog-R; rep from * around.

Row 24: *C3L; rep from * around.

Row 26: *K2tog-L, k1; rep from * around.

Row 27: *C2R; rep from * around.

Row 29: *K2tog-L; rep from * around.

Row 1: K4, p2, *RC8L; rep from * to last 2 sts, k2.

Row 2 and all WS rows: K4, *p2, k2; rep from * across.

Rows 3 and 7: K4, *p2; k2; rep from * across.

Row 5: K2, *RC8R; rep from * to last 6 sts, k2, p2, k2.

Rep rows 1–8 for pat.

instructions

SIDEBAND

With larger needles and waste yarn, CO 112 (128, 144, 160) sts using a provisional method (page 115). PM and join.

Change to project yarn and work in rnds 1–8 of Chart 1 for a total of 24 (32, 32, 40) rnds.

Cont working rnds 9–29 of chart until 14 (16, 18, 20) sts rem.

Next (dec) rnd: *K2tog-R; rep from * around—7 (8, 9, 10) sts.

Next (dec) rnd: Knit, dec 1 (0, 1, 0) sts evenly around—6 (8, 8, 10) sts.

Next (dec) rnd: *K2tog-R; rep from * around—3 (4, 4, 5) sts. Cut yarn, draw tail through rem sts and secure.

Return to provisional CO row and turn hat inside out, WS facing—this will be the RS of the piece when working the chart. Carefully remove waste yarn, place 112 (128, 144, 160) sts on smaller needle, PM between sts 6 and 7 of rnd to mark beg of Side Flap 1.

SIDE FLAP 1

With larger needle, work in Chart 2 over next 24 (32, 32, 40) sts, turn.

Next and all WS rows: K2, work in pat to last 2 sts, k2. Work in pat for 15 rows, ending with a WS row.

Next row (RS): *K1, k2tog-R, k1; rep from * across—18 (24, 24, 30) sts. Cont along left edge of flap, pick up and knit 12 sts to provisional CO.

FRONT FLAP

Cont along provisional CO sts, work Chart 2 over next 32 (32, 40, 40) sts, turn. Work as for Side Flap 1, ending with row 16.

With right needle, pick up and knit 12 sts along right edge of Front Flap to match sts picked up along left edge of Side Flap 1.

Next row (RS): *K1, k2tog-R, k1; rep from * across—24 (24, 30, 30) sts.

Cont along left edge of flap just worked, pick up and knit 12 sts down to provisional CO sts.

Rep last two flaps to create Side Flap 2 and Back Flap of hat, picking up 12 sts along each flap edge where directed—180 (192, 204, 216) sts on needle, ending at corner of a side flap.

With smaller needle work I-cord BO (page 118) around lower edge of hat and around flaps, graft ends tog.

FINISHING

Weave in ends. Block. Fold up Front Flap and tack in place.

Triangular Wedge Hat

materials and tools

Artyarns Cashmere 5 (100% cashmere; 1.75oz/50g = 102yd/93m):
(A), 1 skein, color gray blue variegated #1005; (B), 1 skein, color blue
variegated #107—approx 204yd/186m of medium weight yarn

Knitting needles: 4.5mm (size 7 U.S.) 16"/41cm circular and double
pointed needles or size to obtain gauge

4.5mm (size G U.S.) crochet hook

Stitch markers

Tapestry needle

gauge

25 sts/36 rows = 4"/10cm in pat

20 sts/28 rows = 4"/10 cm in St st

Always take time to check your gauge.

finished measurements

Approx 19 (22)"/48 (56)cm circumference

A fun and intriguing knit, this hat features two knitted triangles that come together to form the base. Both triangles use the same stitch pattern, but on opposite sides, creating a different texture for each piece.

design by
Nichole Reese

skill level
intermediate

assembly diagram

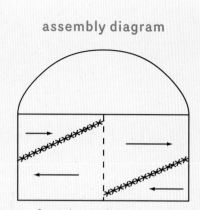

×   Sew selvage edges

--   pu sts for Triangular Wedge 2

instructions

TRIANGULAR WEDGE 1

With A, CO 31 (37) sts.

Rows 1 and 3 (RS): K1, *p1, k1; rep from * across.

Rows 2 and 4: P1, *sl 1, p1; rep from * across.

Row 5: K1, ssk, *p1, k1; rep from * across—1 st dec.

Rows 6, 8, 10: *P1, sl 1; rep from * across.

Rows 7 and 9: K2, *p1, k1; rep from * across.

Row 11: K1, p2tog, k1, *p1, k1; rep from * across—1 st dec.

Row 12: P1, *sl 1, p1; rep from * across.

Rep rows 1–12 until 3 sts rem, then work rows 1–4 once more. BO. Sew tip of triangle to right corner of CO edge.

TRIANGULAR WEDGE 2

With RS facing and B, pick up and knit 29 (35) sts along rem CO edge of Triangular Wedge 1.

Rows 1 and 3 (WS): K1, *p1, k1; rep from * across.

Rows 2 and 4: P1, *sl 1, p1; rep from * across.

Row 5: K1, *p1, k1; rep from * to last 3 sts, k2tog, k1—1 st dec.

Rows 6, 8, 10: Sl 1, *p1, sl 1; rep from * to last st, p1.

Rows 7 and 9: *K1, p1; rep from * to last 2 sts, k2.

Row 11: K1, *p1, k1; rep from * to last 3 sts, p2tog, k1—1 st dec.

Row 12: P1, *sl 1, p1; rep from * across.

Rep rows 1–12 until 3 sts rem, then work rows 1–5 once more—2 sts.

Next row: P2.

Next row: K1, p1.

Rep last 2 rows once more.

Next row: P2. BO. Sew rest of triangles tog.

SHAPE CROWN

NOTE: *Change to dpns when needed.*

With A, pick up and knit 104 (108) sts around top of band formed by triangles. PM and join. Knit 4 rnds.

Next rnd: *K2, k2tog; rep from * around—78 (81) sts.

Knit 5 rnds.

Next rnd: *K1, k2tog; rep from * around—52 (54) sts.

Knit 5 rnds.

Next rnd: *K2tog; rep from * around—26 (27) sts.

Knit 5 rnds.

Next rnd: *K2tog; rep from * to last 0 (1) sts, k0 (1)—13 (14) sts.

Knit 1 rnd.

Next rnd: *K2tog; rep from * to last 1 (0) sts, k1 (0)—7 (7) sts. Cut yarn, draw tail through rem sts and secure.

FINISHING

Weave in ends. With crochet hook and B, work 1 rnd sc around lower edge of hat. Fasten off.

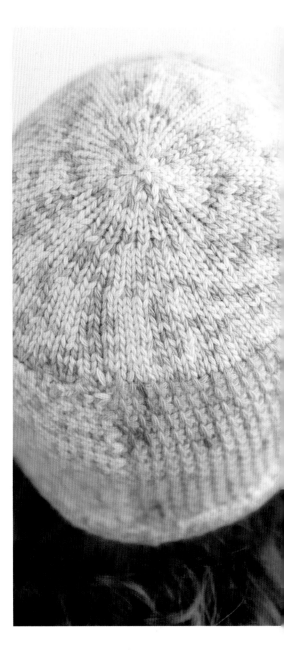

Pinstripes have always been effective, and this sideways knit beret allows the gentle colors of the hand-dyed yarn to work together and create this stunning result.

design by
Woolly Wormhead

skill level
intermediate

Sideways Pinstripe Beret

materials and tools

Artyarns Cashmere Sock (67% cashmere, 25% wool, 8% nylon; 1.75oz/50g = 160yd/146m): (A), 1 skein color green and rust variegated #1008; (B), 1 skein, color taupe tonal #2305—approx 320yd/292m of fine weight yarn ⓶

Knitting needles: 3mm (size 2½ U.S.) straight needles or size needed to obtain gauge

Waste yarn

Stitch marker

Tapestry needle

gauge

26 sts/32 rows = 4"/10cm in St st

Always take time to check your gauge.

special abbreviation

W&t: Wrap and turn; see Short Rows with Wraps on page 122

finished measurements

15 (17¾, 20)"/38 (45, 51)cm circumference

pattern chart

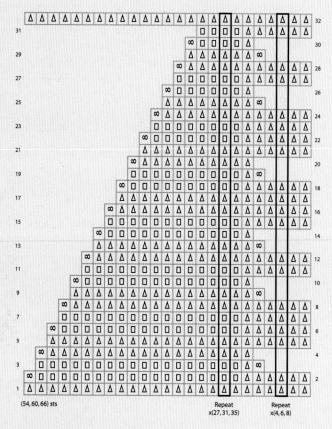

(54, 60, 66) sts

Repeat x(27, 31, 35) Repeat x(4, 6, 8)

△	With A, knit on RS, purl on WS
▢	With B, knit on RS, purl on WS
∞	wrap and turn the next st, leaving the wrapped st on left working needle

instructions

PANEL

Using crochet provisional cast-on and A, CO 54 (60, 66) sts.

Row 1 (WS): With A, purl.

Row 2 (RS): With A, k9 (11, 13); with B, k44 (48, 52), w&t.

Row 3: With B, p44 (48, 52); with A, k1, w&t.

Row 4: With A, k43 (47, 51), w&t.

Row 5: With A, purl.

Row 6: With A, k9 (11, 13); with B, k42 (46, 50), w&t.

Row 7: With B, p42 (46, 50); with A, p9 (11, 13).

Row 8: With A, k50 (56, 62), w&t.

Row 9: With A, p42 (46, 50), w&t.

Row 10: With A, k1; with B, k40 (44, 48), w&t.

Row 11: With B, p40 (44, 48); with A, p9 (11, 13).

Row 12: With A, k48 (54, 60), w&t.

Row 13: With A, p40 (44, 48), w&t.

Row 14: With A, k1; with B, k38 (42, 46), w&t.

Row 15: With B, p38 (42, 46); with A, p9 (11, 13).

Row 16: With A, k46 (52, 58), w&t.

Row 17: With A, purl.

Row 18: With A, k9 (11, 13); with B, k36 (40, 44), w&t.

Row 19: With B, p36, (40, 44); with A, p1, w&t.

Row 20: With A, k36 (40, 44), w&t.

Row 21: With A, purl.

Row 22: With A, k9 (11, 13); with B, k34 (38, 42), w&t.

Row 23: With B, p34 (38, 42); with A, p9 (11, 13).

Row 24: With A, k42 (48, 54), w&t.

Row 25: With A, p34 (38, 42), w&t.

Row 26: With A, k1; with B, k32 (36, 40), w&t.

Row 27: With B, p32 (36, 40); with A, p9 (11, 13).

Row 28: With A, k40 (46, 52), w&t.

Row 29: With A, p32 (36, 40), w&t.

Row 30: With A, k1; with B, k30 (34, 38), w&t.

Row 31: With B, p32 (34, 38); with A, p9 (11, 13).

Row 32: With A, knit across all sts, picking up the wraps as you go—54 (60, 66) sts. Rep rows 1–32 a total of 6 (7, 8) times, omitting last row on final rep.

FINISHING

Carefully remove provisional CO and place on needles. Join to live sts using Kitchener st.

NOTE: *When grafting across short rows, pick up the wrap from the RS and place it on the needle, then lift both the wrap and st off and twist toward you, then place back on the needle and work Kitchener st as normal; this keeps work in pat. Thread yarn through crown sts and pull to tighten. Weave in ends.*

Block carefully.

Bias Slouchy Hat

materials and tools

Artyarns Supermerino (100% superwash merino wool; 1.75oz/50g = 104yd/95m): (A), 1 skein color blue variegated #107—approx 104yd/95m of medium weight yarn

Artyarns Rhapsody Light (50% silk, 50% kid mohair; 2.75oz/80g = 400yd/366m): (B), 1 skein color blues #H3—approx 400yd/366m of lightweight yarn

Knitting needles: 4.5mm (size 7 U.S.) straight needles or size to obtain gauge

Waste yarn

Stitch marker

Tapestry needle

gauge

20 sts/32 rows = 4"/10cm in St st using A

20 sts/36 rows = 4"/10cm in k1, p1 rib using a double strand of B

Always take time to check your gauge.

finished measurements

16 (18, 20)"/41 (46, 51)cm circumference

This is a fantastic hat for demonstrating the qualities of, and differences between, two different weight yarns. The bias effect plays on these properties, creating this beautiful slouchy fit piece.

design by
Woolly Wormhead

skill level
intermediate

pattern chart

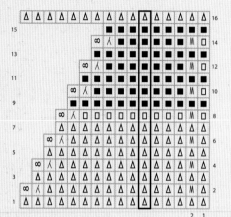

(33, 36, 39) sts

Repeat
X(18, 21, 24)

△	With A, knit on RS, purl on WS
■	With B, purl on RS, knit on WS
□	With B, knit on RS, purl on WS
∞	wrap and turn the next st, leaving the wrapped st on left working needle
M	M1 on RS knit rows, M1P on RS purl rows
Ʌ	k2tog on RS knit rows, ssp on RS purl rows

instructions

NOTE: *Use a single strand of A throughout. On the body of the hat, use a single strand of B. Use a double strand of B on the brim.*

BODY PANEL

CO 33 (36, 39) sts using crochet pro-visional CO (page 115).

Row 1 (WS): With A, purl.

Row 2 (RS): With A, k1, M1, k29 (32, 35), k2tog, w&t.

Row 3: With A, purl.

Row 4: With A, k1, M1, k28 (31, 34), k2tog, w&t.

Row 5: With A, purl.

Row 6: With A, k1, M1, k27 (30, 33), k2tog, w&t.

Row 7: With A, purl.

Row 8: With B, k1, M1, k26 (29, 32), k2tog, w&t.

Row 9: With B, knit.

Row 10: With B, p1, M1p, p25 (28, 31), ssp, w&t.

Row 11: With B, knit.

Row 12: With B, p1, M1p, p24 (29, 30), ssp, w&t.

Row 13: With B, knit.

Row 14: With B, p1, M1p, p23 (28, 29), ssp, w&t.

Row 15: With B, knit.

Row 16: With A, knit, picking up wraps—33 (36, 39) sts.

Rep rows 1–16 a total of 8 (9, 10) times. On the last rep, omit row 16.

JOIN BODY

Carefully remove provisional CO and place on needles. Join to live sts using Kitchener st.

NOTE: *When grafting across short rows, pick up the wrap from the RS and place it on the needle, then lift both the wrap and st off and twist toward you, then place back on the needle and work Kitchener st as normal; this keeps work in pat. Thread yarn through crown sts and pull to tighten. Weave in ends. Orient piece so that A sections have the purl side showing.*

BRIM

With B held double, pick up and knit 96 (108, 120) sts around lower edge of hat. PM and join.

Next (dec) rnd: *K2tog, (p1, k1) twice, ssp, (k1, p1) twice; rep from * around—80 (90, 100) sts. Work in k1, p1 rib for 2¼ (2¾, 3 ¼)"/5¾ (7, 8¼) cm.

Bind off using the stretchy bind-off in 1 x 1 rib stitch (page 119) to ensure a truly elastic edge.

FINISHING

Weave in ends. Block.

Interlocking Cloche

materials and tools

Artyarns Cashmere Sock (67% cashmere, 25% wool, 8% nylon; 1.75oz/50g = 160yd/146m): (A), 1 skein color pistachio #191; (B), 1 skein color pale grey #272—approx 320yd/292m of fine weight yarn (2)

Knitting needles: 2.75mm (size 2 U.S.) 16"/41cm circular and double pointed needles or size to obtain gauge

3.25mm (size 3 U.S.) double pointed needles or size to obtain gauge

Stitch holder

Stitch marker

Tapestry needle

gauge

24 sts/28 rows = 4"/10cm in band pat on larger needles

28 sts/40 rows = 4"/10cm in brim pat on smaller needles

Always take time to check your gauge.

finished measurements

20½"/52cm circumference

The Roaring Twenties had a softer side, and this elegant cloche embodies it. While the cashmere gives the hat warmth and softness, the nylon gives it support and shape. The interlocking band offers a bit of playfulness. The hat begins with the band, and the cap and brim are built from its edges.

design by
Amy Micallef

skill level
intermediate

instructions

BAND

With larger needles and A, CO 21 sts. Work in St st for 14 rows.

Row 15 (RS): K7, (k1, M1) 7 times, k7—28 sts.

Row 16: P7, (p1, place next st on holder to the front of the work) 7 times, p7.

Rows 17-28: Work in St st.

Return to sts on the holder, work in St st for 12 rows.

Return to main piece.

Row 29: K7, working three-needle join (page 120), knit the next 7 sts from the holder with the live sts, k7—21 sts. Work in St st through row 180.

Row 181: K7, (k1, M1) 7 times, k7—28 sts.

Row 182: P7, (p1, place next st on holder to the front of the work) 7 times, p7.

Rows 183-206: Work in St st.

Return to sts on the holder and work in St st for 12 rows.

Place this strip of through the loop made on the 1st end worked and return to main piece.

Row 207: K7, working three-needle join, knit the next 7 sts from the holder with the live sts, k7—21 sts. Work in St st for 4 rows. BO. Weave in ends.

With smaller circular needle and B, pick up and knit 144 sts along the top edge of the band (with the end of the crossed pieces pointing downward), PM. Work in St st for 23 rnds.

SHAPE CROWN

NOTE: *Change to dpns when needed.*

Rnd 24: *K10, k2tog; rep from * around—132 sts.

Rnd 25 and every other odd rnd: Knit.

Rnd 26: *K9, k2tog; rep from * around—120 sts.

Rnd 28: *K8, k2tog; rep from * around—108 sts.

Rnd 30: *K7, k2tog; rep from * around—96 sts.

Rnd 32: *K6, k2tog; rep from * around—84 sts.

Rnd 34: *K5, k2tog; rep from * around—72 sts.

Rnd 36: *K4, k2tog; rep from * around—60 sts.

Rnd 38: *K3, k2tog; rep from * around—48 sts.

Rnd 40: *K2, k2tog; rep from * around—36 sts.

Rnd 42: *K1, k2tog; rep from * around—24 sts.

Rnd 44: *K2tog; rep from * around—12 sts.

Rnd 45: *K2tog; rep from * around—6 sts. Cut yarn, draw through rem sts and secure.

BRIM

Place hat on the head with the interlocking pieces over the desired ear.

PM at center of forehead.

Row 1: With smaller circular needle and B, pick up and knit 18 sts on either side of the marker—36 sts. Cut yarn.

Row 2: Pick up and knit 6 sts before the beg of row 1 and knit across live sts. Pick up and knit 6 sts after the end of row 1, cut yarn.

Row 3: Pick up and knit 6 sts before the beg of row 1 and knit across live sts. Pick up and knit 6 sts after the end of row 2, cut yarn.

Row 4/Rnd 1: Pick up and knit 6 sts before the beg of row 3. Cont through the rem live sts. Continue to pick up and knit another 100 sts along the bottom of the band to join in the rnd with the first st—160 sts.

PLEASE NOTE: *When you reach the intersecting pieces you will need to pick up the sts from the back of that work as though it were a continuous band.*

Knit 14 rnds.

Next rnd: Purl.

Knit 10 rnds.

FINISHING

Fold hem along purl rnd and sew live sts to inside of brim on WS. Fasten off. Weave in ends.

Flower Hat

materials and tools

Artyarns Cashmere 5 (100% cashmere; 1.75oz/50g = 102 yd/93m): (A), 1 skein color hot pink #286—approx 102 yd/93m of medium weight yarn

Artyarns Beaded Cashmere & Sequins (65%silk, 35% cashmere with glass beads and sequins, 1/75oz/50g = 90yd/82m): (B), 1 skein color red/gold #H7—approx 90yd/82m of medium weight yarn

Knitting needles: 4.5mm (size 7 U.S.) 16"/41cm circular and straight needles or size to obtain gauge

Stitch markers

Tapestry needle

Decorative button

Sewing needle and thread

gauge

16 sts/22 rows = 4"/10cm in St st

Always take time to check your gauge.

special abbreviation

Turn: Switch needles so your right needle is on the left and the left needle is on the right. See page 122 for Short Rows Without Wraps

finished measurement

approx 22"/56cm circumference

Start with the little flower and continuously build the rest of the hat, which can be knitted mainly on straight needles. This uniquely constructed piece is flattering and feminine.

design by
Iris Schreier

skill level
intermediate

instructions

FLOWER

TRIANGLE 1

With straight needles and A, CO 5 sts.

Row 1: Kfb, k1, turn; sl 1, knit to end.

Row 2: Kfb, k3, turn; sl 1, knit to end.

Row 3: Kfb, k5, turn; sl 1, knit to end.

Row 4: Kfb, k7, turn; sl 1, knit to end— 9 sts.

TRIANGLE 2

Drop A, join B.

Row 1: With B, k9, turn. Kfb, ssk, turn; sl 1, k2.

Row 2: Kfb, k1, ssk, turn; sl 1, k3.

Row 3: Kfb, k2, ssk, turn; sl 1, k4.

Row 4: Kfb, k3, ssk, turn; sl 1, k5.

Row 5: Kfb, k4, ssk, turn; sl 1, k6.

Row 6: Kfb, k5, ssk, turn; sl 1, k7.

Row 7: Kfb, k6, ssk, turn; sl 1, k8.

Cont building additional triangles (all attached to previous ones) in the following color sequence:

TRIANGLES 3, 5, 7

Drop B. With A, rep rows 1–7.

TRIANGLES 4, 6

Drop A. With B, rep rows 1–7.

End with Triangle 7 and drop A—9 sts.

HAT BODY

INCREASE SECTION

Row 1 (RS): With straight needles and B, k1, M1L, PM, k1, M1R, (k2, M1L, PM, k1, M1R) 2 times, k1—15 sts.

Row 2: Purl.

Row 3: With A, (knit to marker, M1L, sm, k1, M1R) 3 times, knit to end—6 sts inc.

Row 4: Purl.

Rep rows 3–4, alternating 2 rows of A with 2 rows of B, until there are 75 sts.

MIDDLE SECTION

Work in St st, alternating (2 rows of A, with 2 rows of B) 2 times. Then work 4 rows of A in St st. Slip all markers, maintaining their position.

DECREASE SECTION

Row 1 (RS): With B, (knit to 1 st before marker, PM, sl 2-k1-p2sso) 3 times, knit to end—6 sts dec.

Row 2: Purl.

Rows 3–8: With A, rep rows 1–2.

Rows 9–10: With B, rep rows 1–2.

Rows 11–16: With A, rep rows 1–2.

Rows 17–18: With B, rep rows 1–2.

Rows 19–24: With A, rep rows 1–2—3 sts.

Row 25: With B, sl 2-k1-p2sso —1 st. Fasten off.

FINISHING

With circular needle and A, pick up and knit 86 sts around lower edge of hat. PM and join. Work in k1, p1 rib for 2 rnds. Change to B and work 1 rnd in pat. Change to A and work 2 rnds in pat. With B, BO in pat. Weave in ends.

Twist triangles into flower shape, sewing button in the center to fasten the "petals" in place.

Camouflage Cap

Shield your eyes with the visor that's knitted using double knitting techniques. Wear it in the woods or around town, and enjoy the original styling not often found in knitted hats.

design by
Iris Schreier

skill level
experienced

materials and tools

Artyarns Ultrabulky (100% superwash merino wool; 3.50z/100g = 110yd/101m): (A), 1 skein color burnt red #H11; (B), 1 skein color olives #1003—approx 220yd/202m of bulky weight yarn (5)

Knitting needles: 6mm (size 10 U.S.) straight and 16"/41cm circular needles or size to obtain gauge

4.5mm (size G U.S.) crochet hook

Stitch markers

Tapestry needle

gauge

14 sts/20 rows = 4"/10cm in St st

Always take time to check your gauge. special abbreviations

K1A: Holding both A&B strands in back, k1 with just A

K1B: Holding both A&B strands in back, k1 with just B

P1A: Holding both A&B strands in front, p1 with just A

P1B: Holding both A&B strands in front, p1 with just B

KfbB: Kfb with just B

Turn: Switch needles so your right needle is on the left and the left needle is on the right. See page 122 for Short Rows Without Wraps.

finished measurements

21"/53cm circumference

instructions

BRIM

NOTE: *The visor portion of this hat is double-knitted. See standard double-knitting rules on p 119. Make sure to twist A around B before the last edge st of the row is worked to carry it along.*

VISOR

With straight needles and B, CO 16 sts.

Row 1: KfbB, *k1A, p1B; rep from * to last st, kfb

Row 2: K1B, *p1A, k1B; rep from * to last st, k1B

Row 3: KfbB, *p1B, k1A; rep from * to last st, kfB

Row 4: K1B, *k1B, p1A; rep from * to last st, k1B

Repeat Rows 1-4 2 times—24 sts.

BRIM

Change to circular needles. With B, using knitted CO (page 114), CO 42 sts, and k24 from brim. PM and join, being careful not to twist the sts—66 sts.

Rnds 1-2: With B, knit.

Rnds 3-4: With A, purl.

Rnds 5-8: With B, knit.

Rnds 9-10: With A, purl.

Rnds 11-14: With B, knit.

Rnds 15-16: With A, *k1, p2; rep from * around.

Rnds 17-21: With B, *k1, p2; rep from * around.

Rnds 22-24: Rep rnd 15.

Rnds 25-26: Rep rnd 17.

CROWN

NOTE: *Crown is composed of 6 triangles worked with short rows.*

Change to straight needles. Cut B.

TRIANGLE 1

Row 1 (RS): With A, kfb, turn; sl 1, turn.

Row 2: Kfb, k1, turn; sl 1, k1, turn.

Row 3: Kfb, k2, turn; sl 1, k2, turn.

Row 4: Kfb, k3, turn; sl 1, k3, turn.

Row 5: Kfb, k4, turn; sl 1, k4, turn.

Row 6: Kfb, k5, turn; sl 1, k5, turn.

Row 7: Kfb, k6, turn; sl 1, k6, turn.

Row 8: Kfb, k7, turn; sl 1, k7, turn.

Row 9: Kfb, k8, turn; sl 1, k8, turn.

Row 10: Kfb, k9, turn; sl 1, k9, turn.

Row 11: Kfb, k10, turn; sl 1, k10, do not turn.

TRIANGLE 2

Row 1 (RS): K1, turn; ssk, turn.

Row 2: K2, turn; sl 1, ssk, turn.

Row 3: K3, turn; sl 1, k1, ssk, turn.

Row 4: K4, turn; sl 1, k2, ssk, turn.

Row 5: K5, turn; sl 1, k3, ssk, turn.

Row 6: K6, turn; sl 1, k4, ssk, turn.

Row 7: K7, turn; sl 1, k5, ssk, turn.

Row 8: K8, turn; sl 1, k6, ssk, turn.

Row 9: K9, turn; sl 1, k7, ssk, turn.

Row 10: K10, turn; sl 1, k8, ssk, turn.

Row 11: K11, do not turn.

TRIANGLES 3-6

Rep rows 1–11 of Triangle 2 four more times around. Join the rem 11 sts from Triangle 6 to the 11 rem sts from Triangle 1 using the three-needle bind-off (page 118) on the WS of the hat, forming the top of the crown. Cut yarn, draw tail though the tips of the 6 triangles and secure.

FINISHING

Weave in ends.

Shuti

materials and tools

Artyarns Ensemble (75% silk, 25% cashmere; 3.5oz/100g = 256yd/234m): (A) 1 skein, color gray 247; (B) 1 skein, color green #255 (shown in smaller version) OR (A) 1 skein, color violet #2241; (B) 1 skein, color blues #197 (shown in larger version)—approx 512yd/468m of medium weight yarn (4)

Knitting needles: 4.5mm (size 7 U.S.) 16"/41cm circular and double pointed needles or size to obtain gauge

Stitch markers, 1 in a contrasting color

Tapestry needle

gauge

18 sts = 4"/10cm in double St st

17 sts = 3"/8cm in pat

Always take time to check your gauge.

special abbreviations

DYO: double knitting yarn over, as shown on page 120

WxP: Work x number of pairs in standard double knitting (all pairs match the pair below in color), as described on page 119

LDec (left-slanting dec): Reorder next 2 pairs from KPKP to KKPP as described on page 120; wyib, with A, ssk; wyif, with B, p2tog

RDec (right-slanting dec): Reorder next 2 pairs from KPKP to KKPP as described on page 120; wyib, with A, k2tog; wyif, with B, ssp

Ssp: Sl 2 sts kwise, pass both sts back to left needle, p2tog tbl

finished measurements

18 (21)"/46 (53)cm

This hat utilizes a new technique to adapt lace patterns to double knitting, which gives lace fabric added warmth as well as a built-in background showing through the openwork holes. Work it in two contrasting colors to get the best accent regardless of which "mood" you feel like wearing on the outside. "Shuti" is the name of an Egyptian hieroglyph depicting a two-feathered headdress.

design by
Alasdair Post-Quinn

skill level
experienced

instructions

NOTE: *Work brim 2"/5cm longer if a longer brim that can be turned up is preferred.*

BRIM

With A and B and Double Knit CO (page 116) or double knit cast on of your choice, CO 102 (119) pairs or 204 (238) total sts. PM every 17 pairs, with a contrasting marker at beg of rnd.

Rnd 1: Work 102 (119) pairs, matching colors from the CO rnd below.

Rnd 2: LDec 3 times, (DYO, W1P) 5 times, DYO, RDec 3 times.

Rep rnds 1 and 2 until piece measures 6 (7)"/15 (18)cm from CO edge at beginning of any rep, ending with rnd 1.

SHAPE CROWN

NOTE: *Change to dpns when needed.*

Dec rnd 1: LDec 3 times, W1P, (DYO, W1P) 3 times, DYO, W1P, RDec 3 times—15 pairs rem in each section.

Dec rnd 2 and all even dec rnds: Matching row (W1P to end).

Dec rnd 3: LDec 3 times, (DYO, W1P) 3 times, DYO, RDec 3 times—13 pairs rem in each section.

Dec rnd 5: LDec 2 times, W2P, (DYO, W1P) 2 times, W1P, RDec 2 times—11 pairs rem in each section.

Dec rnd 7: LDec 2 times, W1P, (DYO, W1P) 2 times, RDec 2 times—9 pairs rem in each section.

Dec rnd 9: LDec 2 times, DYO, W1P, DYO, RDec 2 times—7 pairs rem in each section.

Dec rnd 11: LDec, W3P, RDec—5 pairs rem in each section.

Dec rnd 13: LDec, W1P, RDec—3 pairs rem in each section.

FINISHING

Cinch the rem 18 (21) pairs as follows:
Start with the end of B on a tapestry needle. From the facing side of the work, run it through all the loops of A on your needles while keeping it in front of the loops of B. At the beg, run it through 3 more loops of A (one repeat) and remove the tapestry needle.

Put the end of A on the tapestry needle. From the opposite side of the work (working around the inside of the active sts), run it through all the loops of B while keeping it in back of the loops of A. At the beg, run it through 3 more loops of B (one repeat) and remove all needles. Half-knot the ends and feed one through the center, pulling to close. Weave in ends.

techniques

Here are the commonly used techniques in *One + One: Hats*

Casting On

LONG-TAIL CAST-ON

Leaving a tail long enough to cast on the required number of stitches (1 inch per stitch is plenty), make a slipknot and place it on the needle. *Wrap the tail around your thumb and the working yarn around your index finger. Hold the yarn ends with your other three fingers (*figure 1*). Insert the needle into the loop around your thumb from front to back and over the yarn around your index finger (*figures 2 and 3*). Bring the needle down through the loop on your thumb (*figure 4*). Drop the loop off your thumb and tighten the stitch. Repeat from * for the required number of stitches.

KNITTED CAST-ON

This method can be used to begin a project, and it also allows you to add new stitches to stitches you've already knitted. If you don't have stitches on your needle yet, cast on one stitch by placing a slipknot on the needle, and hold the needle in your left hand.

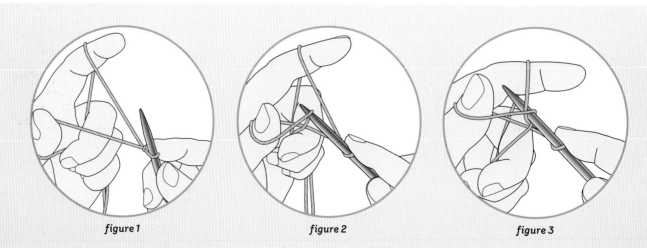

figure 1   *figure 2*   *figure 3*

Insert the right needle into the first stitch on the left needle, as if to knit it. Knit the stitch, but don't drop the stitch from the left needle. Place the newly knitted stitch back on the left needle (*figure 5*). Continue adding new stitches in this manner until you have added as many stitches as the pattern calls for.

PROVISIONAL CAST-ON CROCHET VERSION

A provisional cast-on allows you to knit from both the top and bottom of each cast-on stitch. Once you've knitted a few rows, the stitches can be put back on needles and knitted in the other direction. A smooth, contrasting color of scrap yarn can easily be identified and undone to expose the live stitches.

Using a crochet hook and smooth scrap yarn, chain the number of stitches called for in the pattern, plus an additional five or so. On one side of the chain, the stitches form Vs, and on the other side of the chain, the stitches form bumps. Insert the knitting needle into the bump of the stitch next to the one forming the loop on the hook and knit it (*figure 6*). Continue along the chain, knitting into each following bump, until you have the number of stitches required by the pattern. Now attach the main knitting yarn and start to knit as instructed. After several rows of knitting, or when directed in the pattern, remove the scrap yarn and carefully transfer the live stitches at the bottom edge to a knitting needle. You'll now be able to work these stitches in the other direction.

LONG TAIL PROVISIONAL CAST-ON

Make a slipknot with the working yarn and waste yarns held together and place it on the needle (Slipknot does not count as the first stitch). Adjust working yarn and waste yarn so that waste yarn is draped over your thumb (in the front) and working yarn is draped over your forefinger (in the back). Work long tail cast on. After the next knitted row, slip the slipknot off the needle.

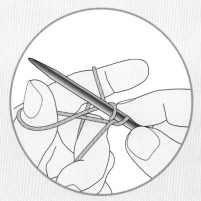

figure 4

figure 5

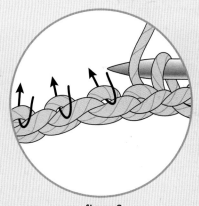

figure 6

UMBILICAL CORD CAST-ON IN WASTE YARN

This technique makes it easier to start at the top of a hat with a small number of stitches. With waste yarn, cast on the specified number of stitches. Work flat in Stockinette stitch for 3"/7.5cm, ending with a WS row. Join working yarn and leaving a 6"/15cm tail, knit one row, dividing the stitches on 3 double pointed needles and join to knit in the round, being careful not to twist the stitches. Follow the instructions for pattern. When ready for finishing, remove waste yarn and place resulting stitches on double pointed needles. Weave the tail through these stitches and pull to close.

TUBULAR CAST-ON

Using waste yarn and long tail method, cast on specified number of stitches. Change to working yarn. Beginning with a row, work 3 rows in Stockinette stitch. On row 4, *p1, k1 from waste yarn by placing left hand needle into the bump of the cast-on stitch from back to front and knitting into the back of the stitch; repeat from * across. This results in double the number of stitches. Remove the waste yarn.

DOUBLE KNIT CAST-ON

This cast-on requires no long tail. Instead, you will be using the long tail technique on the active ends. The nice thing about this is that you get the clean edge usually associated with the long tail cast on without all the tedious guesswork.

To begin, make a slipknot with both colors held together, insert the needle through the loop and tighten. Leave about a 4"-6"/10-15cm tail for weaving in. Don't worry which direction the slipknot colors are facing—you will remove and untie the knot after you complete your first row.

Position your hands. With the needle in your right hand and the tails held out of the way in that hand, put your left forefinger and thumb together and put them between the two hanging active ends. The color hanging over your thumb will be called TC (thumb color) and the color hanging over your finger will be called FC (finger color). In this case, the FC should be your color A and the TC should be your color B.

Close the rest of your fingers over the hanging ends; spread your thumb and forefinger into a Y-shape, and pull the needle back like a slingshot. The ends should come from the needle, pass through the middle of the Y, around each finger from the inside to the outside, and continue down into your closed hand, out the bottom of your loosely held fist, and into your wound source balls.

You will need to differentiate among the four end segments for the next several steps. From the front to the back, you should have the outer TC, the inner TC, the inner FC, and the outer FC.

With your needle in front of all the ends, bring it up underneath the outer TC. Pass the needle over the top of both inner TC and inner FC then down between the inner FC and outer FC. Pull the inner FC down with the needle tip; with that loop of FC on your needle, pass the needle back down between the inner and outer TC ends (the same way you came in) *(figure 7)*. Drop the thumb loop, pick up the hanging end of TC on your thumb again, and tighten. You should have a loop of FC on your needle.

figure 7

Next, you'll do the same thing in mirror image for a reverse long tail cast on stitch. Bring your needle in back of all of the ends.

Bring your needle up from underneath the outer FC. Pass the needle over the top of the inner FC, then down in between the inner FC and inner TC. Pull the inner TC up with the needle tip; with that loop of TC on your needle, pass the needle back up between the inner and outer FC ends (the same way you came in) *(figure 8)*. Drop the finger loop, pick up the hanging end of FC on your finger again, and tighten.

This has created a pair of stitches, the first in your FC and the second in your TC. Continue doing one regular and one reverse long tail cast on stitch to continue alternating cast on colors. I recommend you tighten this cast on a little more than you normally would for a long tail cast on. It will make the first row after the cast on more difficult, but the final edge will be much cleaner.

figure 8

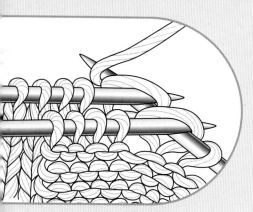

figure 9

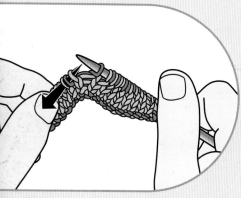

figure 10

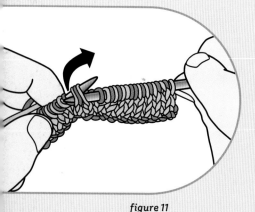

figure 11

Picking Up Stitches

Some projects require that stitches be picked up from the bound-off (horizontal) or side (vertical) edge of a knitted piece. Work with the right side facing you. On the horizontal edge, insert the needle into the first stitch under the bound-off edge and pull a loop through; on the vertical edge, insert the needle between the running threads of the first two stitches and pull a loop through. Continue in this fashion as directed in the pattern.

Binding Off

There are many ways to bind off; here are several techniques used in the book.

THREE-NEEDLE BIND-OFF, OR KITCHENER STITCH KNIT VERSION

The three-needle bind-off is used to join two pieces together while binding off, eliminating the need to sew seams. With the right sides of the knitted fabric that you're joining facing each other, hold the two needles together in your left hand. With a third needle in your right hand, knit two stitches together, working one stitch from the front needle and one stitch from the back needle. *Knit the next two stitches together as before, taking one stitch from the front and one from the back. Pass the previous stitch worked over the latest stitch worked, to bind off. Repeat from * until all stitches have been bound off (*figure 9*).

PURL VERSION

With wrong sides facing outward, place needles with stitches parallel to each other in your left hand. With a third needle, purl the first stitches on each needle together, *purl the first st on each needle together (2 stitches now on the right needle). Lift first stitch over second stitch. Repeat from * until last stitch is bound off.

I CORD KNIT EDGING BIND OFF

To start, cast on specified number of stitches (usually 2 or 3) at start of row/round using a knitted cast on. *K2, ssk, slip 3 stitches from right needle back to left needle. Pull yarn taut across back of work. Repeat from * across until 3 stitches remain, s2kp.

STRETCHY BIND-OFF IN 1X1 RIB STITCH

Work yo (back to front), *k1, pass yo over k1, yo (front to back), pass k1 over yo), p1, pass yo over p1, yo (back to front), pass p1 over yo. Repeat from* across.

Double Knitting

These are the rules of standard double knitting:

All double knitting is worked in pairs. The first stitch in the pair is always the facing-side stitch, is always knit, and is always worked with all active ends in back (wyib). The second stitch in the pair is always the opposite-side stitch, is always purled, is always worked with all active ends in front (wyif), AND is always worked in the opposite color from the facing-side stitch.

In other words, a pair is worked thus:

Wyib, with A, k1; wyif, with B, p1.

DOUBLE KNITTING DECREASES

Both types of single decreases are set up in the same way, in order to reorder 2 pairs from k-p-k-p to k-k-p-p:

The two pairs in the bracket are the two that will be prepared for a decrease. First, insert your right needle purlwise into the first three stitches on the left needle (*figure 10*).

Slip those three stitches onto the right needle. Leave the last stitch in the second pair on the left needle (*figure 11*). You can do this all at once or one by one, as long as you keep them all slipped purlwise.

Insert the left needle into the second stitch on the right needle from the back (*figure 12*). Pull the right needle out of two stitches, leaving the first slipped stitch on the needle. Make sure to hold the base of the loose stitch with your thumb.

Insert the right needle into the loose knit stitch (*figure 13*).

Pass two stitches from the right needle to the left (*figure 14*).

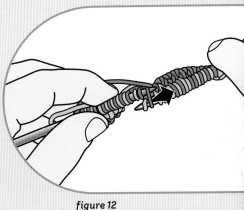

figure 12

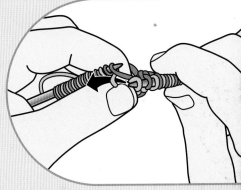

figure 13

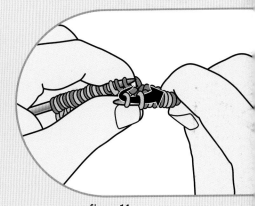

figure 14

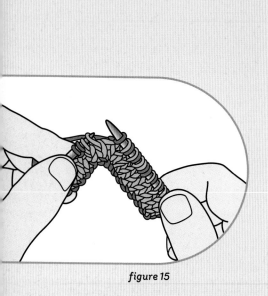

figure 15

The same two pairs are shown here, now reordered for decreasing (*figure 15*).

You can assist figures 12 and 13 with a cable needle to hold the loose stitch, but in general it's not needed for only a single stitch.

Now that your pairs are reordered, your decrease will slant either left or right.

For a left-slanting decrease (Ldec):
Wyib, with A, ssk; wyif with B, p2tog.

For a right-slanting decrease (Rdec):
Wyib, with A, k2tog; wyif, with B, ssp.

DOUBLE KNITTING YARN-OVERS (DYO)

Like regular yarn-overs, double knitting yarn-overs involve wrapping the yarn over the right needle from the front to the back to create a stitch where none was before; after that stitch is worked in the next row or round, a hole is formed below it. Unlike regular yarn-overs, double knitting yarn-overs require you to manage two ends at the same time.

The technique is deceptively simple. Treating the two ends as if they were one, execute a yarn-over, being careful to keep the ends from twisting. Think of the pair of ends as a ribbon, with color A on the right edge and color B on the left edge. Keep the ribbon from twisting as you complete the yarn-over. The ends should already be in the correct orientation to complete the next pair.

Assorted Techniques

THREE-NEEDLE JOIN

Similar to three-needle bind-off, but stitches are knitted together with a third needle from two needles, two stitches at a time, and the number of stitches is reduced by one-half.

WORKING IN THE ROUND

Most large-diameter projects are worked on circular needles in the round. Circular needles for hats are generally 16"–24"/40.5–61cm around at most. Use your favorite method to join in the round, being careful not to twist the stitches and making sure that your working yarn is not inside the circle of stitches. For a clean join you can cast on one extra stitch, then join to knit in the round by slipping the first cast on stitch from left to right, and pass the slipped stitch over the extra cast on stitch. It is good practice to place a marker to identify the start of a round.

When working small-diameter sections in the round, the small number of stitches will no longer fit on circular needles. There are two options:

Double pointed needles (dpns) are commonly used: Place as close to the same amount of stitches on each of 3 or 4 double pointed needles. Knit around using a fourth or fifth double pointed needle. Pull tight to avoid gaps between stitches when switching from one needle to another.

Two circular needles are also used: Just as you would with circular knitting on double pointed needles, you need to distribute the stitches onto the two circular needles as evenly as possible. Work the needles on one end of the circular needle with the needle that is on the other end of that same circular needle. Once all the stitches on the first needle are knitted, continue knitting the stitches on the second needle in the same fashion. Slide them in the proper position to keep them in order. As before, pull tight to avoid gaps between stitches when switching from one needle to the other.

CARRYING YARNS
Here are two scenerios:
When one yarn is used for two rows, it is fairly simple to carry one yarn up along the side when working with the other. Not much thought needs to be given when the yarns alternate every other row.

When yarn is carried along for more than two rows, you will need to fasten the unworked yarn every two rows by twisting it from behind and around to the front of the working yarn. Otherwise the loopy edge will be unattractive and detract from the garment. Make sure not to pull too tightly or leave the yarn too loose. You will need to maintain good tension so that the piece will lie properly.

INTENTIONALLY UNRAVELING STITCHES
To unravel a stitch, simply slide it off your left-hand needle and gently tug on the yarn on either side of the loop until it creates a series of "rungs" of a ladder, going all the way down to the cast on row. This is used in the Drop Stitch Hooded Scarf for the drop stitch effect.

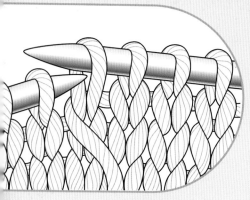

figure 16

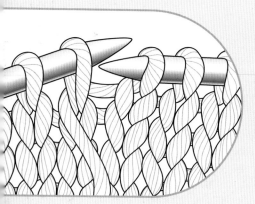

figure 17

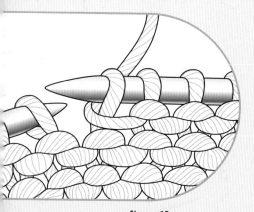

figure 18

FOLLOWING CHARTS IN KNITTING

Some patterns offer charts so that you can visually see how the pattern is formed, whether it is lace or colorwork. Follow each chart round by round (or row by row)—these are always numbered. Repeat the chart the number of times specified in the pattern. Use the key provided to identify what each symbol means. On the colorwork charts, different colors are used to distinguish color A from color B.

SHORT ROWS WITH AND WITHOUT WRAPS

Diagonal short rows with decrease joins do not require wraps, so little needs be said except that it is important to follow the instructions exactly and never stop to take a break in the middle of a row after or before a "turn." Turn by reversing your needles so that the right needle is in your left hand and the left needle is in your right hand. Bring the yarn up and over between the two needles to the back to continue knitting in the other direction. Always take a break only after you have knitted back and you can identify your location in the project. The top of the Camouflage Cap or the flower in the Flower Hat are made with this type of short-row construction.

However, the Sideways Pinstripe Beret, for example, uses short rows that are knitted in a standard fashion. You will find that the instructions tell you to wrap and turn the short rows. Wrap short rows as follows:

If knitting in the pattern, when instructions say "wrap and turn," slip the next stitch purlwise, bring the yarn forward between the needles from the back to the front, slip the same stitch back to the left needle, take the yarn back between the needles, and turn the work to purl back (*figures 16 and 17*).

If purling in the pattern, when the instructions say "wrap and turn," slip the next stitch purlwise, take the yarn between the needles from the front to the back, slip the same stitch back to the left needle, bring the yarn back between the needles, and turn the work to knit back (*figures 18 and 19*).

When all the short rows are worked, smooth the transition between the extra rows and close up the holes from the turns by picking up the wrap along with its stitch on the return row. The technique is slightly different for knit and purl stitches.

If a knit stitch:

Knit to the wrapped stitch. Insert the needle knitwise into the wrap and the stitch that was wrapped; knit them together, dropping the wrap to the purl side of the work (*figure 20*).

If a purl stitch:

Purl to the wrapped stitch. Insert the right-hand needle into the back loop of the wrap and place it on the left-hand needle. Purl the wrap along with the stitch that was wrapped (*figure 21*).

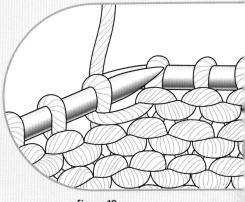

figure 19

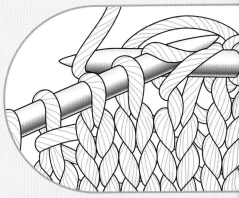

figure 20

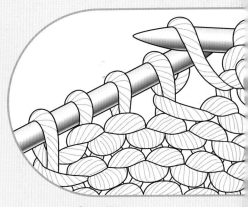

figure 21

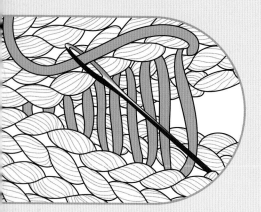

figure 22

figure 23

Finishing Details and Decorative Elements

Here are a few last techniques to finish your projects successfully.

MATTRESS STITCH

A mattress stitch joins two pieces of stockinette in such a way that the knitting appears to be continuous. Use a darning needle threaded with the same yarn used in the project, block the two pieces you are seaming, and hold them side by side with the right sides facing you. Insert the needle under the horizontal bar between the edge stitch and the one next to it, pulling the yarn through the bar, and insert the needle under the matching bar on the opposing piece. Continue in this fashion until you have completed the seam *(figure 22)*.

I-CORD

An I-cord is formed with a special three-pronged gadget, or by simply knitting a few stitches in the round with two double-pointed needles as follows:

Cast three stitches onto one double-pointed needle; do not turn. *Slide the stitches to the opposite end of the needle and hold it in your left hand, with the right side of the work facing you. Draw the working yarn to the right behind the cast-on stitches, and using the second double-pointed needle, knit the three stitches again. Repeat from * until the I-cord is the desired length. As you work, be sure to draw the working yarn somewhat tightly across the back of the stitches so you form an evenly rounded cord *(figure 23)*.

TWISTED CORD TIES

Combine two equal lengths of the two yarns, tying each end with waste yarn. Holding one end, twist the opposite end until the cord starts to double back on itself. **Helpful Hint**: The more you twist the cord, the tighter the cord will be. Once the cord is twisted enough, fold it in half and tie both ends securely together with another piece of yarn. Remove waste yarn ties and trim the ends evenly.

TASSELS

Follow the project directions regarding the exact length and number of strands; one strand should be longer than the others. Insert a large crochet hook into the stitch in which a tassel is to be inserted. Draw one end of the cut strands through this stitch, making sure that they hang evenly on both sides of the stitch (with the exception of one end of the longer strand). Wrap the longer strand around the others five times, securing the tassel around the stitch. Insert a small crochet hook up into the tassel, catch the piece of longer strand that has been wrapping around the tassel, and pull it through so that it hangs down with the remaining strands. Trim if necessary to even all the lengths.

FRINGE

Using the number and length of strands specified in the project, hold the strands together evenly, folding them in half to make a loop. Insert a large crochet hook into the garment where you'll be applying the fringe and catch all the strands in the center.

Draw the loop end through (*figure 24*), making it large enough so you can pull the ends of the yarn through the loop (*figure 25*). Pull down on the ends so the loops tighten snugly around the stitch.

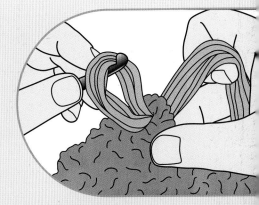

figure 24

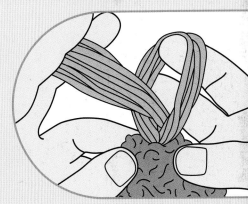

figure 25

About the Designers

TANYA ALPERT

Tanya Alpert, knitwear designer and author of *Haiku Knits*, was born in Eastern Europe (Kiev, Ukraine), and graduated from the Kiev Institute of Art & Design. She first learned to knit at six years old. Since moving to the United States in 1988 she has explored many forms of art including fiber art, jewelry design, and graphic arts. Her fiber art pieces have been shown in galleries around the United States, and her knitting creations have been sold around boutiques in La Jolla and Del Mar, California. Tanya's designs go beyond the traditional. Influenced by nature, her unique collection of knitted designs is modern, simple, and very wearable. Please visit her at http://knittingbythebeach.com and on www.ravelry.com under TanyaAlpert.

LISA ELLIS

Lisa Ellis is a knitwear designer and traveling knitting instructor in the greater Seattle/Tacoma area. Lisa is a contributing designer to over a dozen books and magazines and her patterns can be found in over one hundred yarn shops across the country as well as numerous online yarn stores and catalogs. Her website is www.LisaEllisDesigns.com.

PAM GRUSHKIN

Pam Grushkin is a lifelong knitter who shares her passion for knitting and crochet through teaching and designing. Her designs have been published in *Vogue Knitting*, *Knitting Socks with Hand-painted Yarn*, and independently as *Knits with a Twist*. She lives in Connecticut, where she blogs at www.stitchandchat.blogspot.com.

LISA HOFFMAN

Lisa Hoffman is a yarn artist living in New York City who has published patterns in *Vogue Knitting Magazine* and in the books *Vogue Knitting on the Go: Bags 2* and *Vogue Knitting: Mittens and Gloves*. Fiber and color direct Lisa's designs, and all are garments she herself would want to wear.

DANIELA JOHANNSENOVA

Daniela Johannsenova was born in the former Czechoslovakia. Crafts and especially knitting and sewing were always part of Daniela's life. In 2006, after some of her creations appeared in a German fashion magazine, she decided to open a yarn shop in the city center of Cologne, Germany—Maschenkunst—which has become extremely popular. Daniela's designs are featured in major German magazines, including *Verena Knitting*. She works as a knitwear editor at the family lifestyle publication *Magazín Luna*, where she creates 10 baby and children's collections per year. Daniela is the distributor of Artyarns yarn across Europe. Her website is www.maschenkunst.de.

JUDITH RUDNICK KANE

Judith Rudnick Kane has an extensive art background, holding a BFA and an MA in painting from Hunter College. She worked as a studio artist for many years and her paintings have been exhibited widely; she has taught art, color theory, and knitting at all age and skill levels. Judith is the owner of Yarns for Your Soul LLC, in Manchester, Vermont, and has designed many of the models on display in the shop. Judith also does needlepoint and creates her own colorful canvases.

LAURIE KIMMELSTIEL

Laurie Kimmelstiel is a knitter, weaver, and designer, and founder of the Ethelridge Road Knitting Salon. She is a contributor to a variety of knitting publications and coauthor of *Exquisite Little Knits*. She chronicles her knitting life at http://the-yarn-princess.blogspot.com. Her website is www.whiteridgecrafts.com. Laurie can be reached at knittingsalon@gmail.com.

AMY MICALLEF

Amy Micallef is a fiber artist in Brooklyn, New York. By day, she works as a costume/craftsperson on Broadway. By night, she designs knitwear; works on window displays at La Casita Yarn Shop; and owns Amy's Organbank, where she makes plush, happy, internal organs for people who are missing parts or have parts that need encouragement. In her spare time, she is also the creator of Unstable Mable Stitch Markers, which are composed of horror movie equipment and other silliness: hand saws, butcher knives, zombies, brass knuckles, and happy toast. Amy also loves to crochet, felt, needle felt, quilt, embroider, sew, and can MacGyver any object into something completely different. If you'd like to see more of her work, you can find her at https://www.ravelry.com, as Organbank on Etsy.com, or at her personal website, www.pinkadellic.com.

ANNIE MODESITT

Annie lives, knits, and crochets in St. Paul, Minnesota, with her family. She loves to bike, and when she's not shoveling snow she's usually riding around her neighborhood. Annie knits in the Combination Method and believes there is no wrong way to knit! Her website is www.modeknit.com.

MELISSA MORGAN-OAKES

Melissa Morgan-Oakes was taught to crochet, tat, and sew at an early age by women who encouraged her to work without commercial patterns. She taught herself to spin and knit, designing patterns for her handspun yarns as she went. She brings the unique perspective of a self-taught knitter to her energetic and enjoyable classes and designs. She lives on her small chicken farm in western Massachusetts. Melissa is the author of *2-at-a-Time Socks*, *Toe-Up 2-at-a-Time Socks*, and *Teach Yourself Visually Circular Knitting*.

BROOKE NICO

Brooke Nico began her designing activities by sewing her own wardrobe, inspired by drape and color. She brought her talents to knitting almost ten years ago, first exploring modular construct, then lace. Next, Brooke opened Kirkwood Knittery, a local yarn shop located in St. Louis, Missouri. As a dedicated teacher, she guides knitters through the intricacies of techniques to make their projects as polished as possible.

SINJE OLLEN

Sinje Ollen has been knitting since her childhood (creating store samples for knitting stores in her teens). She graduated from Stella Adler Conservatory of Acting in 1994 (appearances on TV and Broadway) and worked at the New York Stock Exchange for six years (connecting different computer platforms). All of her experiences have influenced and enhanced her knitting, which she continued throughout. Since 2004, Sinje has been exclusively knitting. Her work can be found at www.sinjeollen.com. Kits and patterns are available at www.etsy.com/shop/sinjeollen and at www.ravelry.com/designers/sinje-ollen.

ALASDAIR POST-QUINN

Alasdair Post-Quinn is a lifelong crafter who lives in Cambridge, Massachusetts, with his wife and cat. When he's not knitting, he enjoys cooking; fixes computers for Brandeis University; listens to esoteric music, audio books, and NPR; and tries to spend as much time outdoors as possible. Visit him online at www.double-knitting.com.

NICHOLE REESE

Nichole Reese designs for her company, bluegirl knits, as well as other publications. She teaches at her LYS, Knot Another Hat in the beautiful Columbia River Gorge in Oregon, as well as other venues in the Pacific Northwest. Nichole is an accountant who loves applying her skills in math and efficiency to her designs. You can check out her designs and keep up with her blog at www.bluegirlknits.com.

SHARON SORKEN

Sharon Sorken thinks she was knitting before she learned to walk. She awakes each new day with colorful designs dancing in her head. At her knitting classes, she encourages her students to create their own designs and advance their skills. Sharon's designs and patterns can be found at www.sharonsorken.com and www.ravelry.com.

HEATHER WALPOLE

Heather Walpole is a graphic designer turned yarn "spaz." Her approach to knitting is to create fast, fun-to-knit projects that are meant to be completed in little more than a weekend. Check out her collection of Ewe Ewe Yarns and patterns at www.eweewe.com.

LYNN M. WILSON

Lynn Wilson is a designer, knitting instructor, and dedicated knitter. Her design philosophy is to create patterns that provide knitters with hours of pleasure as they successfully knit beautiful projects. Lynn's designs have been featured in *Knit Simple Magazine, 60 Quick Knits in Cascade 220, 60 More Quick Knits, 60 Quick Baby Knits,* and *Vogue Knitting's on the Go: Bags 2.* She has designed for Be Sweet Yarns and Tanglewood Fiber Creations and has her own collection of Lynn Wilson Designs knitting patterns. More information is available on her website, www.lwilsondesigns.com.

JENNIFER WOOD

Jennifer Wood designs for Wood House Knits. She taught herself to knit ten years ago and loved it so much she began designing her own patterns. It has been a wonderful outlet for her creative energy. She has an absolutely wonderful husband, three amazing children, a fine son-in-law, a sweet, sweet grandbaby, and two bad dogs. Her patterns can be found on her website, www.woodhouseknits.com, and at www.raverly.com under woodhouseknits.

WOOLLY WORMHEAD

Woolly Wormhead is a hat architect. With a background in industrial, sculptural, and fine art textiles, these influences can be seen in her work; having always been a lover of hats and a lifelong knitter, she enjoys bringing these different aspects together. Constantly fascinated with unusual construction techniques, developing stitch combinations and techniques to achieve a unique, versatile piece, Woolly Wormhead is always encouraging knitters and crocheters to be more adventurous. Her website is www.woollywormhead.com.

LAURA ZUKAITE

A native Lithuanian and a graduate from Parsons The New School for Design, Laura is happily pursuing her career as a designer in New York City. The author of *Luxe Knits* (Lark, 2009) and *Luxe Knits: The Accessories* (Lark, 2010), her books feature designs made with exceptional yarns and convey Laura's design philosophy. Just recently she has launched her knitting pattern design website, www.laurazukaite.com, where knitters from all over the world can access Laura's designs with one click.

Photo by: Elliot Schreier

About the Author

Iris Schreier couldn't find the yarn she wanted for her designs and, with the mission of elevating the art of knitting, decided to create it herself. She is the founder of Artyarns, a company that has built its reputation on producing luxurious, sophisticated hand-dyed yarns of the highest quality. Since 2002, Artyarns has offered a variety of special yarns, including merino wool, silk, cashmere, mohair, and has featured fiber blends as well as embellished yarns enhanced with beads, sequins, and gold or silver metallic strands.

Taught by her mother, Iris has been knitting since she was about six years old. She has always been drawn to decorative and fanciful types of projects, and is known best for her unique designs for modular knitting, lacework, and reversible knitwear.

Iris is the author of several Lark books, including *Exquisite Little Knits* (with co-author Laurie Kimmelstiel, 2004), *Modular Knits* (2005), *Lacy Little Knits* (2007), *Iris Schreier's Reversible Knits* (2009), and *One + One: Scarves, Shawls & Shrugs* (2012).

Her original techniques are used in knitting workshops around the world, and her patterns have been translated into various languages. Iris has appeared on the television programs *Knitty Gritty* and *Needle Arts Studio*, and has written articles and published patterns in leading magazines. Visit her Facebook page at http://www.facebook.com/artyarns and see her designs on her websites: http://www.artyarns.com and http://www.irisknits.com.

Acknowledgments

Without the support of the incredible group of designers who contributed to this collection, it would just not have been possible to create this book. You are all terrific! My mom pitched in with last minute knitting and I really appreciate that, as well as the encouragement I received from Elliot, Owen, and Jason, as well as my knitting group friends, during this process. And many thanks to everyone at Lark who has pulled this together, including Amanda Carestio, Amy Polcyn, Meagan Shirlen, Orrin Lungdren, Lynne Harty, Valerie Shrader, and my editor Beth Sweet!

Knitting Abbreviations

ABBR.	DESCRIPTION	ABBR.	DESCRIPTION	ABBR.	DESCRIPTION	ABBR.	DESCRIPTION
[]	work instructions within brackets as many times as directed	kfb	knit in the front and back of the same stitch	prev	previous	sl1k	slip 1 knitwise
()	work instructions within parentheses as many times as directed	KUS	knit under strand	psso	pass slipped stitch over	sl1p	slip 1 purlwise
		kwise	knitwise	pwis	purlwise	sm	slip marker
**	repeat instructions following the asterisks as directed	k2tog	knit two stitches together	p2tog	purl two stitches together	ss	slip stitch (Canadian)
*	repeat instructions following the single asterisk as directed	k3tog	knit three stitches together	p(2)sso	pass (2) slipped stitches over	ssk	slip, slip, knit these 2 stitches together–a decrease
		LDec (left slanting dec)	Set up 2 pairs as follows: wyib, with A, ssk; wyif, with B, p2tog.	rem	remain/ remaining	sssk	slip, slip, slip, knit 3 stitches together
"	inches			rep	repeat		
alt	alternate	LH	left hand	rev St st	reverse stockinette stitch	ssp	slip 2 stitches knitwise, pass both stitches back to left needle, p2tog tb l.
approx	approximately	lp(s)	loop(s)				
beg	begin(ning)	m	meter(s)	RH	right hand	st(s)	stitch(es)
bet	between	MC	main color	rnd(s)	round(s)	St st	stockinette stitch
BO	bind off	mm	millimeter(s)	RS	right side	s2kp/sl 2-k1-p2sso:	Insert needle into 2nd and first stitches as to k2tog, knit the next stitch, then pass the 2 slipped stitches over.
CC	contrasting color	M1:	make 1 stitch	RC8B:	Sl 4 sts to cable needle and hold to back, k2, p2, k2, p2 from cable needle.		
cm	centimeter(s)	M1/ M1L (make 1/ left)	Lift bar between stitches from front to back, knit through the back loop.				
cn	cable needle			RC8F:	Sl 4 sts to cable needle and hold to front, k2, p2, k2, p2 from cable needle.	tog	together
CO	cast on					WS	wrong side
cont	continue	M1p (make 1 purl)	Lift bar between stitches from front to back, purl through the back loop.	RDec (right slanting dec)	Set up two pairs as follows: wyib, k2tog; wyif, ssp.	w&t:	wrap and turn the next stitch, leaving the wrapped stitch on the left working needle
dec	decrease/ decreases/ decreasing			sk:	skip		
dpn(s)	double pointed needle(s)	M1R (make 1 right)	Lift bar between stitches from back to front, knit the stitch.	skp	slip, knit, pass stitch over–one stitch decreased	wyib	with yarn in back
fl	front loop(s)					wyif:	with yarn in front
foll	follow/ follows/ following	oz	ounce(s)	sk2p	slip 1, knit 2 together, pass slip stitch over the knit 2 together; 2 stitches have been decreased	yd(s)	yard(s)
		p or P	purl			yfwd	yarn forward
g	gram					yo	yarn over
inc	increase/ increases/ increasing	pat(s) or patt	patter ns	sl:	slip	yon	yarn over needle
k or K	knit	pm	place ma rker	sl st	slip stitch(es)	yrn	yarn around needle

Needle Size Chart

METRIC (MM)	US	UK/CANADIAN
2.0	0	14
2.25	1	13
2.75	2	12
3.0	—	11
3.25	3	10
3.5	4	—
3.75	5	9
4.0	6	8
4.5	7	7
5.0	8	6
5.5	9	5
6.0	10	4
6.5	10½	3
7.0	—	2
7.5	—	1
8.0	11	0
9.0	13	00
10.0	15	000
12.0	17	—
16.0	19	—
19.0	35	—
25.0	50	—

Yarn Substitution Chart

YARN IN PROJECT	WEIGHT	YARN SUBSTITUTION
Beaded Cashmere	4	Lion Brand Amazing or Glitterspun or Wool or Superwash Merino-Cashmere
Beaded Cashmere & Sequins	4	Lion Brand Amazing or Glitterspun or Wool or Superwash Merino-Cashmere
Beaded Ensemble	4	Lion Brand Amazing or Glitterspun or Wool or Superwash Merino-Cashmere
Beaded Mohair & Sequins	3	Lion Brand Microspun
Beaded Pearl	4	Lion Brand Amazing or Glitterspun or Wool or Superwash Merino-Cashmere
Beaded Silk Light	3	Lion Brand Microspun
Cashmere 1	0	Lion Brand LB 1878
Cashmere 3	2	Vanna's Glamour™ Yarn
Cashmere 5	4	Lion Brand Amazing or Glitterspun or Wool or Superwash Merino-Cashmere
Cashmere Glitter	2	Vanna's Glamour™ Yarn
Cashmere Sock	2	Vanna's Glamour™ Yarn
Cottonspring	3	Lion Brand Microspun
Ensemble	4	Lion Brand Amazing or Glitterspun or Wool or Superwash Merino-Cashmere
Ensemble Glitter	4	Lion Brand Amazing or Glitterspun or Wool or Superwash Merino-Cashmere
Mohair Splash	3	Lion Brand Microspun
Rhapsody Glitter	3	Lion Brand Amazing or Glitterspun or Wool or Superwash Merino-Cashmere
Rhapsody Light	3	Lion Brand Microspun
Silk Pearl	3	Lion Brand Microspun
Silk Rhapsody	4	Lion Brand Amazing or Glitterspun or Wool or Superwash Merino-Cashmere
Supermerino	4	Lion Brand Amazing or Glitterspun or Wool or Superwash Merino-Cashmere
Ultrabulky	5	Lion Brand Wool-Ease© Chunky Yarn
Ultramerino 8	4	Lion Brand Amazing or Glitterspun or Wool or Superwash Merino-Cashmere

Yarn Weights

YARN WEIGHT SYMBOL & CATEGORY NAMES	0 lace	1 super fine	2 fine	3 light	4 medium	5 bulky	6 super bulky
TYPE OF YARNS IN CATEGORY	Fingering 10-count crochet thread	Sock, Fingering, Baby	Sport, Baby	DK, Light Worsted	Worsted, Afghan, Aran	Chunky, Craft, Rug	Bulky, Roving

Source: Craft Yarn Council of America's www.YarnStandards.com

Project Index